QUESTIONEERING

The New Model for Innovative
Leaders in the Digital Age

JOSEPH M. BRADLEY

QUESTIONEERING

The New Model for Innovative
Leaders in the Digital Age

Contents

Section I
The Road to Questioneering

Section II
Becoming a Questioneer

CHAPTER EIGHT
Stay in Tune with Emotion
81

CHAPTER NINE
Leverage Momentum
89

CHAPTER TEN
Cost Cutting: Right Answer, Wrong Question
97

CHAPTER ELEVEN
Create High-Value Answers
109

Section III
Four High-Value Questions

CHAPTER TWELVE
What Do I Say When Silence Is Not an Option?
123

CHAPTER THIRTEEN
Is Securing My Data Trustworthy Enough?
147

CHAPTER FOURTEEN
Job Promotion or a New Level of Fulfillment?
171

CHAPTER FIFTEEN

Will Technology Uplift or Replace the Human Spirit?

203

Notes

224

Figures and Tables

In memory of my grandparents Joseph and Marjorie Goodwill, who taught me the greatest personal reward comes from the joy of giving to others, loving unconditionally, and expecting nothing in return.

Acknowledgments

AS I THINK ABOUT the writing of this book, there are so many people I'd like to thank who have inspired me and given me the opportunity to live a life without limits and to truly dream in an unconstrained way.

I remember my first job. I went to my mom and dad and said I wanted to be a paperboy. I'll never forget it. My dad just gave me this look and said, "You want to be a paperboy? Of all the things that you can come up with, you decide that you want to be a *paperboy*?" I must have been around eleven years old, and I replied, "Well, what else is there?" Dad gave me another challenging look and said, "How about computer programming? You're pretty good at programming, right?"

This was right around the time the first personal desktop computers were introduced onto the market. I had just heard about basic programming, and it seemed pretty cool to me. So, my dad bought a Commodore PET computer with a cassette tape in it. I started teaching myself basic programming and wanted to teach others how to program, too. Dad helped me make a flier that we passed out to people at our church. And before you knew it, I had five or ten students: my first business. I still think about that time with affection. I owe a huge debt of love, gratitude, and respect to my parents because they instilled in me the belief that, through the power of education, you truly can achieve whatever you want in life.

That belief has stuck with me and given me, quite frankly, the motivation to write this book while working full-time and raising my two lovely kids with my wife, Laurie, to whom I also owe a huge debt of gratitude and love. I remember walking into my African American studies class at UC Berkeley my freshman year and sitting in the back of the classroom with a group of friends. Typical of our age and gender, we looked at all these beautiful women walking into class. We started musing, "Would you be able to go out with that person? Could you ask them out on a date?" I remember seeing the prettiest woman I had ever seen in my life. And I said, "Now *that's* a woman whom I could call my wife. That's a woman I can marry."

My friends all just laughed and told me they didn't believe I'd ever actually ask her out. Well, lo and behold, four or five weeks later, Laurie and I were going out. And we've been together for thirty years, including twenty-five years of marriage. We started going out our freshman year and got married a year after we graduated from college. Laurie has been an incredible support; my rock. There's that old saying, "Behind every great man is a better woman." I say, "In front of a great man is a better woman." Laurie is such a remarkable source of support and an amazing wife and mother. It's been an incredible experience loving and raising our children together. I owe Laurie my life and everything I can possibly give her.

From a business perspective, I need to thank Chuck Smith at Pacific Bell, my mentor for well over fifteen years and still my mentor today. Chuck is an outstanding leader who taught me the power of communication (*Communicate! Communicate! Communicate!*) as well as the power of people. I'll never forget that. I've learned so much from him. He motivated me and shaped my leadership style throughout my career. You'll see that focus on communication and the art of storytelling in this book.

Another inspiring leader, motivator, and good friend is John Chambers. A person's character is judged by what they do when no one is watching. When I needed support, John was always there. He could have easily not answered the phone or brushed me aside. But he didn't. John really made a difference and helped me continue along my career path. What a great inspiration! I'll always remember him telling me, "Joseph, don't confuse activity with results. Stay focused and keep pushing."

For more than eight years, I've also had the opportunity to work with and lead what I believe to be the greatest, most talented team in the world. Special thanks go out to James McCauley, Andy Norona, Jeff Locks, and Hitendar Sethi. You're one of the best thought leadership research teams one could ever have. Special thanks also go out to Stephen Miter, Joel Barbier, and Christopher Riberger for being some of the most strategic financial minds I've had the privilege to work with. These guys inspired a lot of the wisdom at the beginning of this book. I also want to thank the world's greatest strategists, Richard Metcalf and Stephen Miter, for again inspiring, challenging, and allowing me to help shape their leadership paths as they grew and as I grew throughout my career.

Another special thanks must go out to Alicia Swanson. Alicia's positive energy and support at numerous conferences and keynotes ensured that my message was on point and the content was where it needed to be. Her immeasurable enthusiasm allows me to present with the highest level of confidence and is reflected in the energy of the crowd. Alicia is one of *the* top marketing professionals I've ever had the chance to work with. She's also a great friend. I really appreciate her support.

And last but not least: a huge thank you to Su Le. Every Batman has a Robin, and from a right-hand perspective, Su has been just incredible. He always took my brainstorming calls at four or five in the morning. When I asked him to pick up and move his family to Chicago, Su didn't hesitate. "No problem," he said, "I'll be there." Whatever I needed, Su was there. He's an incredible thought leader and a great operations executive who truly understands technology. But most importantly, Su is just a great friend.

I've probably missed many folks who've played some part, big or small, in the process of writing this book. To all those named and unnamed, I owe you a huge debt of gratitude and appreciation.

Now without further ado, it is my honor to share with you the art I call Questioneering.

Section I

THE ROAD TO QUESTIONEERING

CHAPTER ONE

Understanding Questioneering

YEARS AGO, MY TEAM and I had an opportunity to work with a retailer with a very interesting question. "Our problem," the store manager said, "is when customers perceive our lines are long, they leave the store. They simply don't want to wait in long lines. When customers see our lines getting longer and longer, they say, 'I'm out of here.' Many abandon simply abandon their carts and leave. Now, not only do we lose the revenues, we have restocking issues. But most importantly, we're losing sales."

In response, I asked my team, "Okay, can we solve this?" But it turns out this was the wrong question.

Unwittingly, we immediately began to search for the answer to the wrong question. We identified what we called dark assets: fixed or mobile assets that, if connected to the store's operational process, could provide data to solve the retailer's problem.

"What do customers do before they even enter the store?" we asked. They park their cars. The parking lot was a dark asset. So, we connected the parking lot. We captured parking events at the street level through various sources, including ground-embedded parking sensors, video coverage, and analytics. We placed sensors in the parking stalls to determine if a car was present or not.

Then we asked, "What do customers do next?" They grab a shopping cart, another dark asset. We added sensors to the shopping carts and used wireless technology to determine their location as customers pushed them through the store. The shopping carts gave us geo-spatial data that helped us understand where each cart was located in the store at a particular point in time. In other words, we were able to understand the path each customer took before they checked out.

Once we identified the dark assets, we asked, "How can we capture the data from these assets?" We took the information from the parking lot sensors and combined it with the data from the shopping carts. We had identified our dark assets and collected our data. All we had to do was implement a change to the retailer's business process. This led us to ask, "Can we apply analytics to change and fundamentally understand when these lines are getting long?"

Sure enough, we could. By knowing the rate of people entering the store and analyzing where they are in the store by the position of their shopping carts, we found we could predict forty minutes in advance when a store would experience long lines. We discovered the milk case was one of the last stops customers took before they went to the cashier. If there was a rush in the milk aisle, we knew a rush at the checkout lines wasn't far behind.

The store was so excited that they wanted to implement the solution right away, before we had an opportunity to complete what I believed was the most important step. But we'll get to that soon enough.

The store manager got excited and cried out, "We've got it! We've got it! We've got the answer!" Before he let me explain the data, he ripped our analysis out of my hands and saw that line seven was about to get long. He grabbed the speakerphone and said over the store intercom, "Hey, Bob. Can you come from the back of the store please and open check stand number seven? Our lines are about to get long. Please come up. Check stand seven."

Now I want you to pause and think a moment about the problem we were trying to solve. What was the question we originally asked? *How can we reduce the amount of time that a customer waits in line?* And what we said is that when customers *perceive* that the lines are getting long, they leave the store. Unfortunately, after all that financial and technological investment, when the manager grabbed the speakerphone and announced to the entire store that the lines were getting long. Customers heard that, abandoned their carts, and left—a self-fulfilling prophecy.

In the end, our innovative technological solution was all for naught. We failed to complete the most important step, connecting to the retailer's darkest asset: people. It's critical in any technology implementation to understand how you'll fundamentally change people's behavior as a result of using the technology. In this case, having the store manager notify employees over the intercom wasn't the optimal behavior. We needed to change this behavior. So, we said, "We solved the problem. Now all we have to do is notify the appropriate store clerk via text message that the lines are getting long. That individual will come now to the front of the store and customers will be none the wiser." And yes, our solution was a success.

Later, I shared this story with my son and daughter, both college students. My son, who was an accounting and computer science major at the time, and my daughter, who was an English and classics PhD candidate, were enamored with the story. My son shared his insights, saying, "You see the power of being a technical major and having a technical degree? Do you see that this is what's enabled Dad to see the value? This is what I want to study when I go to college." And then something very interesting happened. My daughter pointed out that we found the right answer to the wrong question.

She said, "Well, Dad, you actually asked the wrong question."

"What do you mean?" I asked.

"You shouldn't have asked how to reduce the *length* of the lines. Instead, you should have asked, 'How do you eliminate the lines?'"

It's here that the true notion and power of Questioneering was born.

Our Connected World

When I think about technology and how far we've come, I recall my twentieth wedding anniversary, five years ago. My wife and I celebrated with a trip to Hawaii. When we got to the security line at the airport, the TSA agent stated, "Please take out anything that will need to go through the X-ray machine." For some reason, this well-worn phrase got me reflecting. Remember how you had to remove 35-millimeter film from your camera before it went through the X-ray machine?

That day, we removed a deluge of things from our bags: cameras, phones, tablets, and so on. Once we got through the checkpoint, we gathered all our electronic equipment back into our various bags and, after what seemed like a long time, finally headed off to our gate.

That equipment was put to good use very quickly. Within three hours of arriving at the hotel, my wife had taken more than one hundred photos! But not only had she taken these pictures, she had also already uploaded all them online through a shared photos album we use regularly. My dad was on his cell phone as soon as my wife uploaded the pictures, posting comments like, "Oh, I love this photo," and "You should go here, and you should go there." I just sat on our couch in our hotel room marveling at how connected we have become. Here we were in Hawaii while my father, thousands of miles away in California, was communicating in real time about the experience my wife and I were having in Hawaii on our twentieth wedding anniversary.

That's the world we live in today. Every day, the equivalent of fifty years of a human's life is uploaded to YouTube. By 2020, humans will generate fifty zettabytes of data every day. To give you an idea of what that means, fifty zettabytes is the equivalent of twelve and a half *trillion* DVDs of data. And these numbers will continue to grow and grow and grow.

After our trip to Hawaii, I thought about my New Year's resolutions. I told my wife, "Next year, I'm going to embrace the notion of what I believe is digital. In fact, my goal is to become, even though I'm a forty-year-old man, a *millennial.*"

It was a very interesting experience when I dedicated myself to becoming a millennial. I learned two core things that are vitally important to this generation. One, if you're going to be a millennial, the first true test is to ask yourself, "What would I give up before I lost connectivity to the internet?" In 2012, the Cisco Connected World Technology Report found the majority of millennials would actually give up their sense of smell before they lost their connectivity to the internet.[1]

Another thing I learned is that more than half of millennials, if given the option to see a doctor who could implant a chip in their brain with direct access to the internet, would sign up immediately. Again, this is the world we live in. This may become the new concept of being well connected in the digital world.

Our desire for connectivity is only increasing. People once took years to adopt this technology, but now they can be convinced to get further connected in a matter of minutes, if not seconds. It took Wells Fargo bank twenty years, starting in 1995, to acquire 25 million online banking customers. Fast forward to 2005 and the popular app MyFitnessPal, which took only ten years to acquire 80 million users, almost four times the users of Wells Fargo in half the time. Now jump forward to 2011 and the creation of Snapchat; in just four years, the social media company grew to 200 million users.

This is the connected, digital world we live in. It dictates the path to success for both individuals and companies. The stakes are high for everyone.

The Impact of the Answer Mindset on Business Value

As the senior research fellow for the Global Center for Digital Business Transformation, a research organization associated with the Swiss business school IMD, I had an opportunity to drive a significant piece of research with some colleagues. We interviewed approximately one thousand senior business leaders from across the globe. We wanted to understand the notion of disruption in the digital age. Was it something companies and business leaders could simply ignore or was it something that truly matters? To this end, we held workshops and events and conducted in-depth discussions with dozens of startup founders and senior executives. We analyzed well over one hundred disruptors.

We asked the participants, "If you looked at the top ten incumbents in your marketplace over the next five years, how many do you believe would be displaced due to digital disruption? How many will no longer be there?" The group answered four out of ten. Forty percent would no longer fall into the top ten within their respective marketplaces! Then we asked, "Forget the five years. How long do you think this will take to occur?" They responded, "Within three years." That equates to 40 percent of the top ten incumbents being displaced or extinct. More recently, we followed up by asking, "Because this is so important, do you have a plan?" To our surprise, only 25 percent of company executives and top business owners said they had an active plan to address digital disruption.

Therein lies the core issue: four out of ten incumbents will be displaced in only three years, and yet almost none have paused to create a plan to prevent it. Matthew S. Olson and Derek van Bever's excellent book *Stall Points: Most Companies Stop Growing—Yours Doesn't Have To* analyzes five hundred companies in the Corporate Knights Global 100 over the past half-century. The book does a deep-dive analysis of about fifty firms that hit what the authors call a *stall point*. A stall point is a situation where a company that had grown at least 2 percent annually over a ten-year period hits a revenue stall. To count, the difference in growth before and after hitting the stall had to be at least 4 percent, while the company's growth rate after the stall had to be at least below 6 percent. The study looks at what happened to these firms when they hit a significant stall point.

Here's what the authors found. First, more than 90 percent of firms that hit a stall point lost more than half their market value after the stall. The average drop was 74 percent and the average executive turnover was 50 percent. If you're sitting there now saying, "Well, don't worry. This won't happen to me," let me tell you, nine out of ten companies will experience a revenue stall. Put another way, only one out of ten companies will *avoid* a revenue stall. What's more, only one of the nine companies that experience a revenue stall ever recover. Let's put this in practical terms. I'm sure you remember when having a Kodak moment was a good thing. You remember Kodak, don't you? It was one of the original innovating companies in the photography world and the inventor of the digital camera. Well, guess what? This inventor of digital pictures no longer exists (Figure 1).

Kodak

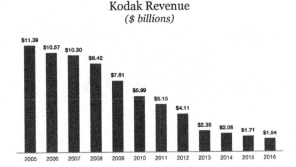

Kodak Revenue
($ billions)

Sources: Kodak company filings, Statista

Figure 1: Kodak

What about Blockbuster? The company promised movies on demand. Then Blockbuster got "Neflixed." Blockbuster went out of business as everyone switched to Netflix and streaming video (Figure 2).

Blockbuster

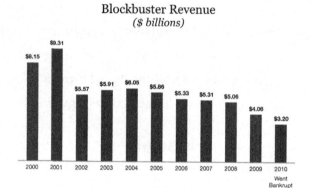

Blockbuster Revenue
($ billions)

Sources: Blockbuster company filings

Figure 2: Blockbuster

Remember Borders bookstores? Amazon arrived on the scene and Borders closed up shop (Figure 3).

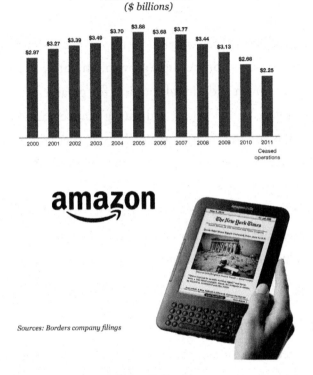

Figure 3: Borders

If you're still sitting there saying, "This isn't going to be me. I know how to get my business out of a revenue stall," you've only got a 10 percent chance of success. Remember, Olson and Bever's analysis found of the nine companies that experience a revenue stall, only one of the nine companies answers the right questions to recover.

The Answer Mindset

The pace of innovation is accelerating at blazing speeds. Whether you search Google or ask Apple's Siri, Microsoft's Cortana, or Amazon's Echo, the digital world provides answers at an exponential rate. Just watch any twelve-year-old doing homework. Siri has turned iPhones (and parents) into answer machines. It all contributes to the biggest obstacle to success: the Answer Mindset.

If you're a product manager trying to improve customer experience, a CEO in search of elusive double-digit growth, an entrepreneur looking to take on Facebook, or an individual looking for greater fulfillment in the digital age, the biggest challenge is dedicating yourself and your resources to what you believe are the right answers. But whether you realize it now or later, many of your current right answers are not right. Why? You've been asking the wrong questions.

The biggest barrier to success in the digital age is that all answers are known. You create value by knowing what questions to ask. This is the learning journey that I've embraced for twenty years and what I'll share with you in this book.

The Secret to Success: Take Time to Question

What's the secret to success in this digital world where the stakes are so high?

Many believe the answer to solving this problem is to say, "The secret to success is action. We have to move. We've got to change our offices to appeal to millennials. We've got to go grab a bunch of pretty yellow and orange stickies. We've got to sit on some cool beanbag chairs with no backing. We've got to play video games in the office. We've also got to take off our suits and throw on jeans, a blazer, and some cool tennis shoes."

Those who embrace the Answer Mindset say, "Don't worry. Let's just get stuff done." If only it were that easy. I've got to tell you, it's not about just getting *stuff* done. It's about getting the *right* stuff done.

All things are important, but not equal. The most important element of driving breakthrough innovation is to ensure that you're asking the higher-value questions. Whatever question you choose to answer frames all the activities after it. If you choose a low-value question, everything that occurs after it's suboptimal. Kodak's choice of how to become a great picture company framed all of its activities around picture quality and film production. A higher-value question was never asked. How do we enable the sharing of experiences? This question leads to a different set of activities that could have resulted in a higher value outcome. If you rush to solving the answer and don't spend time seriously considering the question at hand, chances are you won't maximize value and miss breakthrough innovation opportunities. In other words, if you're aiming at the *wrong* target you'll never hit the *right* one. I find most leaders and professionals in the digital age are simply aiming at the wrong target.

Which brings us to the foundation of this book, if you want to be successful in the digital age you have to avoid the Answer Mindset and embrace the concept I call Questioneering, a new leadership model that provides you with practical frameworks and tools to change your perspective and state of mind, allowing you to discover the high-value questions for the high-value answers.

The Quick-Start Guide to Questioneering

In a digital world where most answers are known, your value is knowing what questions to ask. This is the fundamental definition of Questioneering. Questioneering is a decision-making model that enables digital age leaders to discover the right questions to get to the right answers. It provides leaders with the tools and capabilities to balance data and knowledge with the beliefs they hold to be true. We'll explore this further in the following chapters.

Questioneering is an end-to-end process. It places greater emphasis on ensuring that you're asking high-value questions than spending your time executing the wrong answers. High-value questions ultimately lead to high-value answers. Questioneering addresses both the *art* of asking better questions and the *science* of driving high-value answers.

Section I: The Road to Questioneering

Section I of this book starts with a description of the problem Questioneering seeks to address. You can never achieve breakthrough innovation if you don't understand the power of asking high-value questions. What results is the Answer Mindset, or the obsession with the generation of answers to the wrong questions and expecting groundbreaking results. As you embark upon the practice of Questioneering, there are three golden rules that provide an essential foundation for unleashing the full power of Questioneering in your organization, your team, business venture, or personal life. We'll discuss each of these golden rules:

1. Don't fail fast.
2. Reverse the value flow.
3. Move from diversity to inclusion.

Section II: Becoming a Questioneer

This is the main section of the book that details what Questioneering is and how you can put it into daily practice to drive breakthrough innovation and achieve results you never thought were possible. The book will cover these four important areas:

1. Discover your blind spots to identify your innovation bias and the source of your low-value questions with the Bradley Blind Spot Map.
2. Ask high-value questions to navigate your Bradley Blind Spot Map using the ASK process (Aim, Surprise, and Kindle).
3. Improve your listening skills with the Convergence Edge and leverage it to create a daily routine and formalized structure for listening to

the knowledge transporters of the digital age: data, emotion, and momentum.

4. Executing high-value answers from high-value questions with a method I've used to drive success throughout my career when faced with some of the most challenging opportunities.

Section III: Four High-Value Questions

Section III brings it all together. You'll learn the four high-value questions leaders, entrepreneurs, and individuals should ask themselves in the digital age:

1. What do I say when silence isn't an option?
2. Is securing my data trustworthy enough?
3. Should I seek a job promotion or new level of fulfillment?
4. Will technology elevate the human spirit or replace it?

Without further ado, let's get started.

CHAPTER TWO

Questioneering Golden Rule One: Don't Fail Fast

I'VE ALWAYS BEEN A Lakers fan. I practically grew up with a basketball in my hand, watching Magic Johnson, James Worthy, and Kareem Abdul Jabbar. I was also a fairly good player from a very young age. My dad practiced with me at the park every weekend. He really put me through my paces: dribbling, shooting, and defensive drills.

By sixth grade, I was really good. I hadn't faced anyone I couldn't beat. I was one of only two sixth graders picked to play in my school's All-Star Game with the seventh and eighth graders. Let me tell you, it was a big deal. I remember this one kid who was very fast. He was as fast as I was, which was weird to me. He was literally taking me to the basket every time he touched the ball. I'd get into my defensive stance and—*boom!*—he'd blow past me. *Bam!* There he went again and again and again.

By the end of the first half, he had scored twenty points. We were only playing twelve-minute halves, so that was twenty points in only twelve minutes. At halftime, my dad came over and asked, "Hey, are you having fun?"

"Not really," I replied.

"Have you figured it out yet?" he asked.

I just gave my dad a blank look as if to say, *No, what are you talking about? I haven't figured anything out yet.*

He then said, "You know, listen. He's left-handed."

Still the blank stare. *Huh?*

"He's left-handed," my dad repeated. "That means he's going to fake like he's going right, but he's going left because he's left-handed."

And then it hit me. "Ugh."

I was so used to doing my own thing and getting into the same frame of mind every time I stepped out onto the court that I was playing by rote. I couldn't see the forest for the trees. I'd stopped learning. I wasn't improving.

It wasn't about failing fast or failing slow. Heck, I was failing fast! This kid was beating me every time he got the basketball. I was failing as fast as you can possibly fail. The key was to ask the right questions to uncover the reason I was failing so I could stop as soon as possible. If you don't want to fail—fast or slow—you need to continuously improve your rate of learning. This is the first golden rule of Questioneering.

Fast or Slow, Failing Is Not Fun

None of us aspire to failure. Any type of failure—fast or slow—isn't fun. Yet countless books and consultants have praised the concept of failing fast, arguing that more than anything, we want to avoid analysis paralysis. We're a society that seems to operate on overdrive. Just do it. Just get it done. As a result, many of us embrace the Answer Mindset. We're focused on finding *any* answer, not on asking the high-value questions that will provide high-value answers.

Clients often ask me how they'll know whether they're asking a low-value question or a high-value question. A sure sign that you're asking a low-value question is if you continue to ask the question again and again without it yielding results. I'm absolutely amazed at the number of times people ask me variations of the same question. They'll always ask, "How do we reduce costs every month? Every quarter? Every year?"

The definition of failing slowly is having the same conversation every year: "We're not meeting our numbers. We haven't met our financial objectives, so we need to optimize the business. We have to let some of our people go." That's failing slowly. You don't want to do that.

Failing fast is that same conversation, but every *quarter*, not just every year. That's not a good outcome, either. It's only speeding up how quickly you're failing. It's certainly not improving your rate of learning.

If you find yourself in this position, it's likely you're not asking a high-value question. One of the primary reasons we continuously ask low-value questions is a misunderstanding of what fuels success in the digital age, the misplaced belief that you must focus on failing fast. This led me to discover what I call the first golden rule of Questioneering: Don't fail fast. Instead, improve your rate of learning.

Improve Your Listening Infrastructure

Most people have only two or three listening sources. Maybe you're confident in another person in your organization, or you're listening to your own gut intuition. When you limit your number of sources, you have a higher propensity to experience blind spots, or areas where you're not opening your mind to listen.

With just one or two listening sources, you become a creature of habit. While you think you're embarking on a new initiative, all you're really doing is acting on muscle memory. You're comfortable having the same conversation every year about how to reduce headcount because, consciously or not, you already know exactly what you're going to do.

Building your listening infrastructure is the first key to improving your rate of learning through Questioneering. This is about understanding whom and what you're listening to so you can understand the context of what's being shared.

Several successful entrepreneurs do a good job of building and maintaining their listening infrastructures. One is Michael Bruch, the founder and CEO of the social platform Willow. He says he spends a couple of hours a day using Twitter to stay updated on the news. While he admits it's not good to obsess over what other people are doing, staying informed is important to him.[2]

Entrepreneur Ryan Holmes, CEO of the social media management platform Hootsuite, believes paying attention to the world around you simply makes sense. He says, "I'm not saying leaders have to be experts in social media, but if there's a communication channel where your employees, customers, competitors, investors, partners, and stakeholders are all spending their time, shouldn't you at least make an effort to be there?"[3]

Seek Out the Negative

The second way to improve your rate of learning through the Questioneering model is to seek out the negative. We all have great ideas that we grow passionate about. But then we also have people in our organizations who think differently than we do. Because they don't agree with us, we view them as negative. We don't seek their opinions out. Instead, we look for people we know will give us the positive energy we crave and agree with our ideas.

Seeking positive energy isn't a bad thing. But to truly grow and uncover high-value questions that could lead to true breakthroughs, you need to challenge your own viewpoint. Seeking out the negative will force you to see if you're truly asking the highest-value question possible and help you continually push into that high-value area.

As you seek out the negative, however, be very careful not to hide behind culture. During the Questioneering process, you may miss opportunities when someone on your team objects, declaring, "That's not who we are.

That's not what we do." They'll use company culture as the safe card that tells you, "Hey, your idea is incompatible with how we conduct business. It's incompatible with how we view the world. Therefore, it's going against our culture."

In the digital age, culture is the last sustainable piece of competitive differentiation. Technology can be copied, but organizations believe their culture is something that cannot be replicated. Laying down the gauntlet of culture squelches most Questioneering discussions, even if you believe you're steering yourself in the right direction. Be very, very careful. Don't avoid seeking out the negative due to the false perception that doing so might be at odds with your organization's culture.

It's easy to get trapped in this mindset. We're constantly evolving. We live and work in a hyperinnovative environment. And while you want to maintain the true core values of your culture, when your culture expands into other areas, such as the markets you're already in, pricing, or competitive strategy, it can get dangerous. You may find yourself saying things like, "Hey, we're a manufacturer, not a technology company," or "Our culture's a consumer-oriented culture, not B2B sales." This is the death knell for innovation.

It's not what you don't know that causes you to fail, but what you believe to be true. The value of seeking out the negative in the Questioneering model is the ability to challenge the unchallengeable, to ask what's not being asked, and to say what's not being said.

Seek the Negative: A Case Study

There was a global technology company, whose name isn't required for this story, that had an internet-centric culture. It viewed the world—and its role in it—as a function of the internet. Company leadership would say, "The internet is the answer. What's your question?" This culture extended to how the firm classified competitors. It believed the internet was a technology, and the company saw its competition as existing within the technology space. As the firm began to think about cloud-enabled services and its overall value, it launched an extensive research initiative into how cloud technologies might evolve. The research team identified which tech companies might be at the forefront of this evolution.

What the researchers failed to understand was that cloud computing requires extensive computing capability. By framing the challenge as a technology issue, not one of capacity, the researchers failed to ask the critical high-value question. They asked, "How can we compete against technology companies?" when the high-value question they should have asked was, "How can we compete against companies that have excess computing capacity because capacity is one of the core capabilities required for cloud computing?" The company was blinded by its culture.

Because of this oversight, no one at the company ever anticipated online retailer Amazon would be a competitor. Indeed, conversations about Amazon, which is now the leading cloud provider in the world, would have been frowned upon because it would have gone against the company's core beliefs. Culture prevented high-value questions from being asked.

Don't get me wrong. Culture plays a valuable role in defining the type of people you want in your organization. Value-oriented qualities such as diversity and innovation are important, but when you expand culture into areas that are more specific to markets, pricing, and competitors, you get into trouble. Seeking out the negative must be fully embraced or you'll perpetually fall into the trap of not challenging what you believe to be true, which will ultimately lead to failure.

Action-Oriented Learning

Tom Chi, one of the founders of Google X, tells a story about the importance of rapid prototyping. Tom was on one of the design teams for

Google Glass, the augmented reality eyeglasses Google developed that display information within the wearer's field of vision.

At the time, most virtual reality goggles were very heavy. Tom's team spent days debating why this was the case. They thought the discussion would help them come up with the right design for their product. After days of futile deliberation, Tom said, "We can stop debating this, guys, and we can just figure this thing out."[4]

He went out to the grocery store to buy some loaves of bread. He plied the wires from the bread bags into glasses frames. Then, his team used balls of clay as weights on different points of the frames. Employees tried them on and gave the team feedback.

The team found that wearers perceive how heavy a pair of glasses is based on how much weight they sensed on the bridge of their nose. When the Google team moved the weight to the back of the earpieces, it took pressure off the bridge of the nose. This gave the perception that the glasses were very light.

By acting to discover the proper weight configuration instead of continuing to debate, Tom and his team found the answer in a matter of hours, if not minutes.

To improve your rate of learning, stop analyzing and learn by doing. Go directly to your customers. The ability to try something to see if it works is critical. Remember, all things are important, but they're not equal.

This is the final key of the Questioneering model: replace debate with action-oriented learning. Action-oriented learning helps you avoid analysis paralysis. To be sure you're taking the right action (which is critically important in an environment where the stakes are high), spend some time ensuring that you're asking the high-value questions to improve your rate of learning. Questioneering forces you to ask the high-value questions so you can learn from the experiment. That's the value.

Now onto the second golden rule: reverse the value flow.

CHAPTER THREE

Questioneering Golden Rule Two:
Reverse the Value Flow

THERE WAS A TIME when I had the opportunity to lead the rollout of high-speed data services—DSL—for the state of California. I ran a center of approximately one thousand employees who ensured the DSL lines that went into our customers' homes worked properly so the customers got what they paid for.

It was common for customers to call our center when they were having issues with their high-speed connection. We wanted to deliver on our promise that our connection was the fastest and most reliable. As a leader, I wanted to make sure that as a company, we were doing everything we could to ensure our customers were getting the service they were promised, and that we were answering their questions. So, I participated in what we called a ride day. I listened to live customer calls as they came in. Three in particular left such an impression on me that I remember them to this day.

Each call had to do with RC Mac. All three customers complained that this guy, RC Mac, hadn't installed their lines properly. And they wanted to know what we were going to do about it.

The thing is, RC Mac wasn't a technician in the organization. He wasn't even a person. RC Mac was the name of an organization that handled line assignment. Basically, they decided which copper pairs were going into which homes to enable the high-speed connection. RC Mac was a partner of ours. How would a customer know about RC Mac or that it was at the root of their connection problem?

I'm sure you've gone into a store to buy a pair of shoes, for example, and the employee says something like, "Hey, you don't need to buy your shoes here. Go buy them down the street. You'll get better shoes for less money." Basically, the employee is referring you to a competitor.

That's what happened with RC Mac. Our employees were so frustrated with us as leaders not asking the right questions, they began to take their frustration out by sharing the details of their discontent with our customers.

Reverse the Value Flow

Why do employees feel the need to refer customers to a competitor? Because leadership never gives them an opportunity to be heard. In most cases, leaders ask good questions, but not high-value ones, limiting their ability to listen and learn. This brings us to the second golden rule of Questioneering: reverse the value flow.

Most discussions about value creation focus on the need to drive shareholder value. You drive shareholder value by creating great experiences for your customers. Most leaders believe they achieve this primarily by deeply and authentically engaging with their customers. Attracting a world-class workforce is secondary. However, the opposite is true.

Value is created primarily by taking care of your employee base. Give them what they need and ensure that they have all the tools, the freedom, and the flexibility to be able to continuously ask better questions to help your organization create a great customer experience.

Corporations don't make bad decisions. They don't decide to move in and out of markets. People do. Adding shareholder value starts with your employees. If you take care of your employees, in turn, they'll take care of your customers. And if they take care of your customers, your customers will drive value to your bottom line. The financials are an output, not an input, just as shareholder value is an output. It's a result of driving value, first with your employees and then with your customers. Your goal is to reverse the conventional corporate-value flow.

Reversing value flow may seem like an obvious solution on paper, but many leaders are blind to it. If you ask business executives or entrepreneurs to tell you what their biggest challenges are, they'll talk about revenue growth, competition, and changing customer expectations and trends. I have yet to hear someone focused on the highest-value question: *what happens when the very best employees leave?*

Putting Knowledge in Context

Leaders have struggled with the notion of knowledge management for a long time. Most have tackled knowledge management by investing in some type of technology. It's usually a program that requires your team to input metatags or metadata into your operational system. But technology alone rarely improves knowledge retention.

Yet many leaders stop there. They haven't considered the high-value questions to lead them to understand how knowledge management offers value. Consider what happens when a top-performing team loses its top players—the Cleveland Cavaliers without LeBron James, or Amazon without Jeff Bezos. Where do the championships go? Where does the innovation go?

Information or data without context is just data. It's like having a bunch of answers everywhere with no way to find them. Context is key. Context is what turns data into information. Questioneering allows us to provide context around the answers knowledge management tools provide. If your knowledge management tool constantly captures answers without providing the appropriate context, the knowledge does not get realized. Your team does not know how to put it in proper context.

High-value questions reveal the most useful and relevant information. They provide context that leverages both better questions and answers. Through the Questioneering process, your team comes to understand how to most effectively apply the data they receive.

Creating a Questioneering Wall

Etymologist and poet John Ciardi believed, "A good question is never answered. It's not a bolt to be tightened into place but a seed to be planted and to bear more seed toward the hope of greening the landscape of idea."[5]

One of the best ways to reverse the value flow within your organization is to create a Questioneering Wall in a high-traffic location in your office. Encourage your employees to write an ongoing series of questions around a challenge or a concern facing your organization. You may include a high-value question as a prompt, such as *What's the best question you've ever been asked and why?* You can break the question out by key categories or key functions in your organization.

You might ask, *What's the best question you've ever been asked around customer experience? Or supply chains? Or sales, marketing, or finance?* By continuously posting high-value questions—no answers, mind you—to this wall, the questions your employees respond with should evolve into the high-value questions that will most benefit your organization. These high-value questions will, in turn, focus your efforts on your core values and the questions you should be asking. The Questioneering Wall is an important part of your listening infrastructure. It captures both your employees' knowledge and the context for that knowledge. But most importantly, it's a powerful way for your employees to feel heard and ultimately provide an excellent customer experience, creating value for your organization.

The Questioneering Wall is an essential step in reversing the corporate value flow. Take care of your employees first and foremost. Once you have, trust them to engage and take care of your customers, and your customers will drive the bottom-line financials in your business. Knowledge management is a great first step in terms of putting your employees first. Questioneering provides a great foundation upon which to do that.

Move Decision-Making Closer to Your Customer

A major technology transition called edge computing is happening right now. Today, most devices gather your information, but the major computing occurs in the cloud. This requires an internet connection. When you ask Siri a question, she accesses the internet or the cloud to give you an answer. Communicating with the cloud takes time.

Edge computing dictates that as we advance further into the digital age, devices and machines will need to make important decisions without delay. They may not have time to access the cloud or the internet. If your self-driving car must decide whether or not to stop for an object or person in a crosswalk, it must reach a conclusion in milliseconds. You can't wait for your car to send data to the cloud to be processed and returned so the car can make a decision. By then, it could already have hit something or someone. Edge computing solves this issue by eliminating the gap between devices and the cloud. Computing is done as close as possible to the data source. For Questioneering to be most effective, it must be performed as closely as possible to the customer. You can't sequester it in upper echelons of leadership.

In most companies, management is at the center of decision making. Decision making must move closer to the customer. For Questioneering to take hold in your organization, you must empower your employees with the ability to ask questions and make decisions. This is critical. You must apply the philosophy of edge computing to your leadership style and your teams. As a leader, you need to think about how you can push decision making as close as possible to your customers, because this is where key learning takes place and true listening happens.

Think of it this way: prior to Questioneering, to be successful in the digital age, you had to think of yourself as a coach. You start every game creating very specific plays for your team to run. When you call out a play, your players perform a defined set of movements based on what you called. When you call X, everybody executes X. This is the way most organizations are run today. When you call X, your people execute X. It's call and response—the Answer Mindset.

Now imagine not asking your team to perform a single play, but arming them with a set of plays to choose from depending on what's happening on the court. When your players have the ball, they can choose the play to make. They might choose to dribble, pass, or drive and score. Or they may replace a teammate's location on the court.

Rather than telling your players to do this or do that, you gave them a set of governance models to apply. How did you come up with those models? You listened to your players and assessed how they reacted and engaged with the other team on the court. This is Questioneering. Your players represent your employees. The other team's players represent your customers.

If you listen to how your employees engage with your customers, you'll understand and ask high-value questions that will help you gain an emotional connection with your customers. And as you improve your questions—continually asking *high-value questions* —you'll create a set of learning principles that you can then impart to your organization. These principles keep corporate knowledge intact and scalable.

This brings us to the third way Questioneering can ultimately help you reverse the corporate value flow and put employees first. Rather than asking why something failed, ask a very important, high-value question: *why did it succeed?*

Using Questioneering to Engage People, Scale Success

I once had the opportunity to work with a real estate broker who was having a very difficult time. While he had always performed well, he was never able to break into the top 10 percent of brokers in his very large firm. So, he asked himself, *what do I need to do to break into the top 10 percent?*

"Aha!" he exclaimed. "I know what it is. I need to focus on my low performers. My bottom-performing groups are really struggling." What he found by talking with these low performers was that they weren't putting in the time to really understand the real estate contract. And because they lacked this understanding, they weren't able to negotiate great deals for their clients.

The second thing he noticed was that the low performers didn't have a good grasp of the local market. They weren't going on broker's tours. They weren't seeing the new homes coming onto the market and therefore didn't have a good sense of the overall marketplace.

The last thing he noticed was that these low performers were failing to make an emotional connection with buyers. They weren't asking high-value questions that would help them develop emotional connections with their clients. They never enjoyed any return business. Each deal was one and done.

My client spent most of the next quarter working with his low performers. And sure enough, they started to understand the contract. They started going to broker's tours and developing emotional connections with their buyers. As a result, their performance improved. They had gone from talking to one client a month to talking with one or two clients a day. My client was really pumped! This is all great.

Then, the results for the quarter came in. My broker friend was convinced he was finally going to break into the top 10 percent. Unfortunately, it turned out to be his worst-performing quarter ever. I asked him, "Why did you focus on the low performers? Why didn't you focus on understanding what made your best performers great? How can they even be better?"

Because he spent most of his time focusing on the low performers, the top performers started to slack off. They started to think that all the work they were doing—all the extra effort they made—wasn't important. Because he stopped praising them, his top performers lost their motivation and drive. My broker friend had focused on what was broken, not what had been successful.

One of the key things Questioneering allows you to do is ask those high-value questions. More often than not, high-value questions focus on how you can scale success rather than how you can fix a problem. There are many reasons why this may be, but I think it's all about positive energy and engagement. Typically, engaged people are successful people. They're energized. Their minds are open.

And because they're energized, excited, and want to share, they're open to the notion of thinking about why something is successful. When they see how high-value questions lead to success, it becomes contagious to ask more of them.

People don't wake up in the morning and say they want to fail. I can guarantee your bottom performers don't come in every day and say, "Man, I can't wait to be one of the bottom performers." Of course not! They want to be at the top. They want to understand what's going on. They want to ask, "What can I do? How can I get there as well?" Focusing on scaling success and on what's working achieves greater success.

If you've ever played a sport, you know winning solves a lot of problems. When you're winning, everything feels a lot better than it is. But when you're losing, everything hurts a lot more than it really should. Because of the Answer Mindset, I think the biases we have as leaders make us want to immediately start looking to fix the problem without really understanding its underlying causes.

I'm challenging you now to understand this bias. I want you to tip the scale and ask high-value questions to uncover why something succeeded as opposed to why it failed.

We're now about to embark upon the last golden rule. We've discussed the importance of improving your rate of learning and reversing the corporate value flow by focusing on your employees, who will in turn pass on this knowledge and care to your customers, who will drive value for your business and shareholders.

But the last golden rule may be the most valuable rule of all.

CHAPTER FOUR

Questioneering Golden Rule Three: Diversity Is Not Enough

HERE WE ARE: THE last golden rule of Questioneering.

Several years ago, a company hired me to lead its inclusion and diversity initiative. Their leadership team asked me to join them on a video conference call to discuss a critical issue. They got everyone together so all voices could be heard, as they were going to make a very important decision. A low-cost competitor who had just entered the market was undercutting the pricing of a service my client traditionally priced at a premium. The call was to create a game plan as to how to respond. Should they announce a price reduction of their service, or should they react in some other way? The high-value question they were trying to answer was, ultimately, *how should we respond to this new competitor?*

At the start of the call, one of the directors said to me, "Joseph, we have really embraced the value of diversity, as you can see. We have leaders from engineering, marketing, finance, strategy, operations, and sales here today. We'd love for you to help us with this dialogue."

The meeting lasted about an hour. As it was ending, one of the leaders said, "I think we have an answer. Based on the conversation we've had today, clearly we should reduce our price in the face of this low-cost competitor. Joseph, you've heard the discussion. You can see that we've really embraced the value of diversity. So, what are your thoughts?"

I looked at the group, all of them anxiously waiting for me to agree that they had come to the right decision. I replied that there was no doubt the company had brought together a diverse group of leaders and viewpoints. But then I pointed out that if they were really listening to the conversation, they would haven't noticed that only two voices dominated the entire call. And although they had many diverse individuals on the call, I didn't believe every participant was comfortable in verbalizing or expressing their views.

So, I suggested, "Why don't we try a more inclusive approach? Let's take a poll." The video conference service allowed us to do this in real-time. I quickly created an anonymous poll of all the leaders on the call. I asked, "Do you agree with the recommendation of reducing the price in the face of this low-cost competitor? If you're opposed, what would you recommend instead?"

I gave them about five minutes. When we got the results back, sure enough, the two people who had dominated the call voted in favor of lowering the price. But, the other eight who hadn't spoken up had completely opposing views. The call extended for another thirty minutes and a decision was reached to not lower pricing and instead pursue a strategy of increasing the perceived customer value of the solution.

Now imagine what would have happened had we ended the conversation with the two dominant participants pushing to lower pricing. We've all been in those meetings: "Let's go with option A." This is an example of the Answer Mindset and demonstrates the difference between diversity and inclusion.

Diversity is the *potential* to create value by having broad range and representation of ethnicity, gender, physical ability, and viewpoints in your company. Inclusion, however, is the *realization* of that value through the full collaboration, participation, and interaction of your diverse workforce.

Ten people sitting in a room looking at each other doesn't create any value, regardless of how diverse that group is. On the other hand, bringing together ten people who are all actively engaged, listening, and participating in the discussion does create value. Remember, at the core of Questioneering is the importance of building your listening infrastructure. If we're all listening to the same point of view, the chance we'll ask high-value questions is very low. You must expand your ability to listen and move from diversity to inclusion.

Inclusion isn't just the right thing to do; it's the profitable thing to do.

Inclusion: The Fuel for Questioneering

Many leaders talk about the power of diversity, and while it's absolutely necessary, diversity on its own isn't actualization. That's not the high-value function. The high-value function is inclusion.

Inclusion is the fuel for Questioneering. It drives the listening infrastructure. Inclusion is the ability for us to achieve the full participation within our organization that creates the true power of that *aha!* moment, of having that high-value question that leads to that high-value answer, and ultimately to that breakthrough innovation.

At Cisco, I partnered with our chief diversity officer at the time, Shari Slate, to launch a study on the effects of diversity and inclusion in organizations. We measured the level of inclusion based on the ability of an employee to feel free to share their views, ultimately driving up participation. We found 93 percent of inclusive organizations exceeded their return on investment expectations for technology investments, as opposed to a 28 percent return for noninclusive organizations.[6]

While diversity is certainly important and necessary, inclusion is the higher-order function. Inclusion is the realization that ultimately drives you to create a very strong listening infrastructure.

Why is inclusion so important to the whole art of extracting value from Questioneering? The following are three core reasons inclusion is an advantage:

1. It maximizes focus on building value.
2. It creates emotional involvement.
3. It drives execution of your strategy.

Inclusion Maximizes Focus on Building Value

I had an opportunity to participate at a function hosted by a primarily African-American organization that promoted African Americans in the field of technology and in technology leadership roles. At this conference, we talked about the role of an IT leader in driving the transformation of an organization. This is clearly an important topic that ranges across multiple companies in multiple facets and isn't limited to African Americans. One of my colleagues, a CIO who was Caucasian, asked if he could attend. I said, "Absolutely. This event is open and welcome to all."

We got there and began to socialize with everyone before the event started. There were probably fifty to seventy-five leading CIOs and IT professionals there, predominantly African American. Members of every culture have their way of greeting one another. In the African-American community, an embrace is a common form of greeting. So, we were embracing and asking each other, "How's it going? How's your family?" I noticed my Caucasian colleague looked uncomfortable. He was normally a gregarious guy. I asked him, "Hey, I noticed you're a bit uncomfortable. Is everything okay?" He looked at me, and knowing that we have a great relationship, he said, "You know, Joseph, to be honest with you, I'm just a little bit uncomfortable because I'm the only Caucasian here." So, I pulled him aside, and I said, "Hey, you know what? It's totally fine."

I reassured him that it was okay to feel a little bit uncomfortable. It's okay to be in touch with your feelings. I said, "What you're experiencing, though, is what many people of color feel when they walk into an environment where they're the only person of color."

Whether you're a woman walking into an all-male environment or someone entering a room dominated by one particular ethnic group, you end up spending a significant amount of time, brain power, and energy asking yourself how to fit in and assimilate. Your focus isn't on asking high-value questions or even on the topic at hand. You stop focusing on building a listening infrastructure, but rather on how you fit in. How do you assimilate? How do you feel comfortable?

If your employees perceive your company culture as noninclusive, you're losing the potential and value of full participation of all those employees. Furthermore, you're fundamentally losing out on the opportunity to ask high-value questions that will take you to a new level of innovation and your breakthrough moment. In the digital age, you need every possible advantage.

Think about all the times when you've stepped into a team that has already been established. How long does it take for you to feel comfortable creating and providing input? Does it take you an hour? A week? A month? A year? In the digital age, a year is like seven or ten years in the real world.

Inclusion is the right thing to do. It's the profitable thing to do. It's also the productive thing to do, the *high-value* thing to do.

Inclusion Creates Emotional Involvement

I've had the opportunity to coach several basketball teams. One of the things I learned very early on is that if I could get my team to be emotionally committed to something greater than the individual good, and buy into the collective team concept, success beyond my wildest imaginations was achievable.

I once coached a high school team where none of the players made the All-Star Team. Yet, that year, we won three tournament championships and made it to the league finals. My players were emotionally committed to doing something and being a part of something greater than themselves.

Inclusion leads to greater emotional involvement. The sky is truly the limit when your employees engage and become emotionally connected to high-value questions. Highly engaged employees have a personal motivation to go above and beyond whatever they originally thought was possible.

In an inclusive organization, full participation across all your employees allows you to stay in the moment and continue to ask increasingly higher-value questions. But how do you know they're high-value questions? Because the energy in the room elevates. And when the energy in the room elevates, you get a high level of emotional attachment, which drives full participation, which then promotes high-level questions that inspire greater engagement. The cycle begins again.

Inclusion Drives Execution of Your Strategy

One of the biggest assumptions we face when we work from an Answer Mindset is that everyone has executed what we've told them to execute. That's how we decide if something was successful: we ask the question, *did it work?*

But a high-value alternative would be, "Did our people engage with each other to execute this strategy?" Think about it. If you're the captain of a ship, and you tell your crew to steer the ship right, but only half your oarsmen turn the ship in that direction, chances are the ship isn't going to turn right.

Now, imagine that you believed your ship had indeed turned right, only to find when you get to your destination that you aren't where you thought you were going to be. You're not where you intended because you didn't drive your team to work together. They never achieved alignment. You didn't lay the groundwork for the precise level of execution where everyone on your ship worked together to give it the opportunity to succeed.

This brings us to the second advantage experienced by inclusive organizations. Inclusive organizations drive engagement, which in turn drives alignment and, ultimately, uniform execution of your strategy.

In an inclusive organization, people engage when they feel that their voices have been heard. If they feel they haven't been heard, they disengage. Disengagement leads to hallway conversations, leading no one being on the same page. High-value questions may very well be asked in the hallway, but since employees are disengaged, no one is learning from those conversations. Their listening mechanisms have been turned off.

Inclusion encourages everyone in the organization to engage and get behind something, which then allows you to have clear alignment. Without full engagement, you can't gain alignment. And if you don't have a team that's aligned to your strategy, there's no way to ascertain whether your strategy is executing according to plan.

One thing you'll find with Questioneering, and the reason why full engagement is so critical, is that there's more than one right answer. In school, we're taught that there's only one right answer, so we search and analyze, and we look for that one right answer. In the real world—in the digital age—there are multiple ways to drive success. That's the power of constantly asking increasingly higher-value questions. What you're ultimately trying to do is gain engagement and alignment to make sure that everyone is fully dedicated and engaged in driving toward your common goal.

As a business leader, it's up to you to lead your organization from diversity to inclusion. As an individual, it's up to you to extract the most value you can from interacting with the world and seeking out that level of inclusiveness.

The point is, you've got to have everyone in the organization committed to asking and driving those higher-value questions.

Section II

BECOMING A QUESTIONEER

CHAPTER FIVE

The Bradley Blind Spot Map: ASK the Right Question

ALBERT EINSTEIN ONCE SAID that if he had an hour to solve a problem, he'd spend fifty-five minutes thinking about the problem and only five minutes thinking about the solution. But in the digital age, we don't follow Einstein's wisdom. Instead, we implement more of a ready-fire-aim technique to solve key business problems. Consider last year's five key business challenges, according to *CIO Magazine*:

1. Organizational resistance to change.
2. Lack of clear vision for the digital customer journey.
3. Ineffective gathering and leveraging of customer data.
4. Inflexible technology stack and development processes.
5. Marriage to the legacy business model.[7]

Though many business leaders generate many different answers to everyday issues, very few take the time to think about what questions to ask—the high-value questions that will lead to high-value answers. The result? Companies consistently experience failure asking low-value questions leading to the wrong answers.

Think back for a moment to the retail story I shared in Chapter One. My client and I realized we shouldn't have focused on the length of the lines at checkout, or even on how to reduce the length of those lines. Rather, we should have focused on the elimination of those lines altogether. The story ultimately illustrates why business leaders in the digital age need to realize that most problems come with blind spots. Then, we need to learn how to identify those blind spots so we can become more successful at finding solutions more quickly.

Remember Circuit City? They had blind spots, including their inconvenient store locations, their slow expansion into gaming, and finally, their lack of in-store partnerships with key, experienced industry leaders such as Apple. Circuit City thought their mandate was to simply sell electronics at their physical store locations. They didn't understand that the true question they needed to ask wasn't how to sell *products*, but rather, how to sell an *experience*. The result? Circuit City is no longer in business. There's a long list of other companies failing to ask the right high-value questions.

How about Toys"R"Us (Figure 4)? It thrived in the 1980s and 1990s because its concept for specialty megastores aligned with the surge in American consumption. In its heyday, Toys"R"Us gobbled up competitors by driving them away the competition. What happened? It continued to ask the *same questions* rather than *high-value* questions that would get to the right answers. Meanwhile, retailers such as Amazon, Walmart, and Target revolutionized the online shopping experience. Toys"R"Us has been in a turnaround since 2004 which was unsuccessful and the company is now in bankruptcy.

Toys R Us

Toys R Us Revenue
($ billions)

			$13.79	$13.60	$13.90	$13.90	$13.50				
		$13.05						$12.50	$12.36		
$11.15	$11.33									$11.80	$11.54
2005	2006	2007	2008	2009	2010	2011	2012	2013	2014	2015	2016

Walmart >¦<

Sources: Toys R Us company filings

Figure 4: Toys"R"Us

This low-value questioning process isn't limited to retail. Sun Microsystems was a computer startup that built high-end servers just as the computer revolution was ramping up. Sun Microsystems talked up the virtues of networking and the universal software they created to run on any computer. Their Java programming language was introduced in the mid-1990s and became an industry standard just when the internet arrived. What was the problem? As PCs became more powerful, fewer big customers needed Sun's costly servers. As a result, they spent most of their time downsizing and retrenching.

What was the question they thought they were trying to answer? Sun was trying to answer the question, "How do we build the best servers?" rather than "How do we deliver computing power?"

Think back to the business challenges listed in *CIO Magazine*. The fifth key business challenge—"Marriage to the legacy business model"—was a major contributor that prevented Sun from recognizing and asking the high-value question of how can customers efficiently gain access to computing power.

A Personal Brush with Blind Spots

I was at the start of my career. I had just accepted a position out of UC Berkeley to become part of the Advanced Management Program for Pacific Bell. It was my first real job after college. I was responsible for managing the finance organization associated with a business unit in their Sacramento office. In this capacity, I needed to articulate what they were spending and how they were adhering to their budget.

My first day on the job, I was introduced to my senior finance manager. He opened his computer to a Lotus 1-2-3 spreadsheet. Lotus 1-2-3 was impressive software with many functions and capabilities and a command-line interface. It came with a big, thick training manual, too.

I spent my first day trying to absorb this information and without feeling overwhelmed. As I picked up to leave the office, I noticed a single cubicle light still on. I walked over to introduce myself. The guy worked in the IT department and had a different spreadsheet on his computer.

This spreadsheet had a graphical-user interface that was activated by a mouse. I was immediately struck by how streamlined and elegant this user interface was. It made me actually *want* to create spreadsheets! I wanted to learn everything about it. It got me energized and excited. I stayed there until one o'clock in the morning exploring its many unique features.

The program was Microsoft Excel. Now, when I look back on that moment, I realize that was the moment I decided I was never going back to Lotus 1-2-3. Even if Excel only had 20 percent of the functionality associated with Lotus and didn't show me how the platform worked as Lotus did,

Excel's graphical user interface inspired me to use it. And that's what I did.

Today, Excel is the dominant spreadsheet application and is fundamentally used in every business and even in our personal lives. Everyone has used or come across someone who has used it. It's also likely the single most important business application ever created, and yet, at the time I chose to switch to it, Lotus controlled the market.

But it didn't for long. Lotus had fallen to its more popular competitors by the early 1990s and formally axed in 2013. What did Lotus not see? As I look across my twenty years in technology, I've come to realize that breakthrough moments in innovation happen when people challenge themselves to continually ask better questions that identify and address their blind spots. When a company is unable to do this, it's inevitably doomed to fail.

If you want to be a successful leader in the digital age, you must develop skills to uncover your blind spots. Companies don't ask poor or even wrong questions. It's the individuals within the companies who don't see what these questions are or don't know how to create better questions that generate results. When I think about how much time we spend seeking great results by asking compelling questions, I think of Einstein, who said, "Most people spend less than 10 percent of their time phrasing the problem they're solving and 90 percent of the time putting it into action, answering the question."[8] This is where mistakes happen. The solution is to flip this process upside down—to spend 80 percent or more of your time figuring out the questions that will better address the problems that exist in your organization and the rest of the time on high-value solutions.

The Bradley Blind Spot Map

If you're fundamentally trying to hit a target and you're lined up aiming to the right, you'll never hit it. To remedy this, I created the Bradley Blind Spot Map. This map will give you a working framework to identify and address your ongoing blind spots. It's a leadership model that will help you understand how to apply 80 percent of your time to ensure that you're asking *better* questions—high-value questions—and 20 percent of the time answering them.

In a study at William Howard Taft University, researchers used an electroencephalograph (EEG) to detect what became known as the Eureka Experience.[9] This is the moment when the fog surrounding a problem clears and you get that *aha!* moment where insight hits. In the study, the researchers presented their test subjects with statements that made no apparent sense, resulting in them being understandably confused. But five seconds later, the researchers gave them a single word that clued them into what they were talking about. As a result, the participants experienced an *aha!* moment.

One of the seemingly nonsensical statements the researchers made was, "The dinner was uneaten because the wood was warped." They paused and then said, "Chopsticks." Less than a half a second later, electrodes attached to the subject's forehead right above their frontal lobes picked up a pulse that came with that flash of insight. Subjects responded with exclamations such as, "Ah, yes! I get it! I understand why the dinner was uneaten—they were eating with warped wooden chopsticks. I get it!"

That same type of *aha!* moment was what I experienced during the retail line reduction experience in Chapter One. I realized I should have asked myself the question, *how do you eliminate the lines?* When I said that, I'm sure many of you reading this got that *aha!* moment as well. That's the Eureka Experience the researchers were studying. They found a period of confusion not only led to insight, but also helped the subjects remember what they had learned. They called the transition from non-comprehension to sudden insight the Memory Boost. You remember it, you get engaged, and you get this jolt of energy to continue to go forward.

That period of confusion of working things out and dedicating your time to that process is why I created the Bradley Blind Spot Map. It'll provide you with the ability to work through and identify your blind spots so you can give yourself the opportunity to have moments of innovation. When I think back over my twenty years of successes and failures in the enterprise segment, whether working at Pacific Bell, Cisco, or HCL or in the startup world at Uptake and C3 Communications, the ability to develop a model to understand your blind spots was flat-out critical.

Your Blind Spot Map

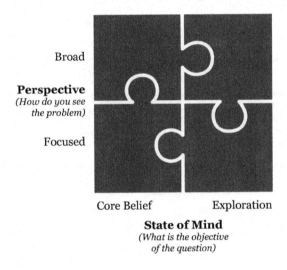

Figure 5: Bradley Blind Spot Map: Perspective

The Bradley Blind Spot Map illustrates two distinct areas where leaders often form Blind Spots (Figure 5). The first is your Perspective. Ask yourself, *is my Perspective Focused or Broad?* In other words, do you tend to think about the details, or do you tend to want to look at the bigger picture?

One way to determine this is to think about how you go about solving problems. Do you tend to start with the details or the big idea? Another good way to identify your Perspective quadrant is to think about what bothers you most when you're sitting in a meeting. Are you more likely to complain about getting dragged into the weeds or about things being too general and not specific enough?

If you're more comfortable taking a Focused approach—getting into the details of things—you have a Blind Spot for a Broad Perspective. In contrast, if you tend to take a Broad Perspective, you have a Blind Spot for a Focused Perspective.

Your Blind Spot Map

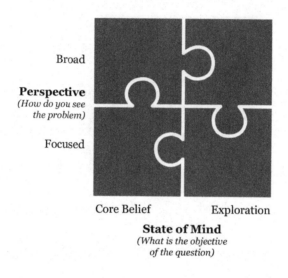

Figure 6: Bradley Blind Spot Map: State of Mind

The second area is your State of Mind; in other words, your core objective (Figure 6). When you're in a meeting and start discussing processes, such as for billing or your customer experience, do you tend to say, "Hey, we should change this process in this manner," or are you more apt to say, "We should implement an entirely *new* process?" If you prefer to change the current process, then your State of Mind favors the Core Belief quadrant, creating a Blind Spot for Exploration. However, if you prefer to implement a new process, you favor Exploration, with a Blind Spot toward the Core Belief quadrant.

When you align your favored Perspective and State of Mind, you'll fall into one of the four quadrants, revealing your Blind Spot. Your job in Questioneering is to figure out how to fill in the other three pieces of the puzzle—the ones you can't see because of your Blind Spot.

A Real-Life Blind Spot Example

Blind Spots came to light in a Fortune 100 company as it pondered an important question regarding its strategic direction related to capturing value from the explosive growth of the Internet of Things (IoT). The IoT is the connection of millions of devices to the internet. The company had a long history in technology and engineering, which led to a Core Belief favoring value from engineering and a Focused Perspective with little appetite for discussing a Broad view. This initially led the company to adopt a strategy that captured value from the IoT.

Fortunately, a colleague and I recognized the Blind Spots and explored a Broad Perspective and Exploration State of Mind. This led to an *aha!* moment where we realized the value from the IoT was in the people using the things, not the things themselves. The bottom line was that you can connect as many things to the internet as possible, but if you don't let people interact with the data and/or change the process, then no value is created. Thus, the Internet of Everything (IoE) was born, proving that value is found in the intersection of people, process, data, and things. Today, the IoE is best known as Digital Business, but the concept is the same.

Your Blind Spot Map

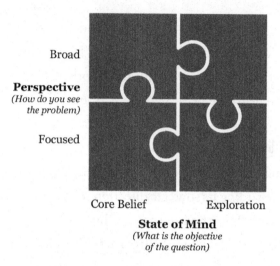

Figure 7: Bradley Blind Spot Map: ASK Process

The Questioneering Process and the ASK Process

In Figure 7, the vertical or Y-axis is what Perspective you bring to a problem: do you favor a Focused Perspective or a Broad Perspective? The horizontal or X-axis represents your State of Mind where you choose whether you already hold a Core Belief or are still in the process of Exploration. Next, let me show you how to use and navigate the map using the ASK Process to ensure you cover your Blind Spots.

The ASK Process helps you and your organization ensure you address one or more Blind Spots rapidly growing in the digital age. The *A* in ASK helps you take better Aim, starting with a deeper and clearer understanding of particular issues or situations. By taking Aim, you ask value-centric questions to more quickly and succinctly understand and define your current Core Belief. Once you've done this, you end up broadening your Perspective around those beliefs and asking high-value, contextual questions.

Next you move on to *S*, or Surprise, where you think about and challenge what you believe to be your organization's core source of value. Here, you expand your horizon of possibility.

And finally, you reach *K*, or Kindle, when you ask questions I call *Why-Why-How* to determine the high-value question that will ultimately lead to a high-value answer.

Before we begin, it's important you know that it's okay to be lost, but don't succumb to the urge to wander. When you're lost, by definition you have a goal you're trying to reach, but you don't know how to get there. That's okay at this point. But it's not okay to simply wander around hoping you'll discover something exciting or new. The essential thing is to be conscious of where you want to go. Let's say you're trying to improve revenue at your organization. You're seeking a better understanding or Perspective around how to create a new business model. You're just not sure what that model is. It's okay not to know at this stage.

Using the ASK Framework to Navigate your Bradley Blind Spot Map A=Aim

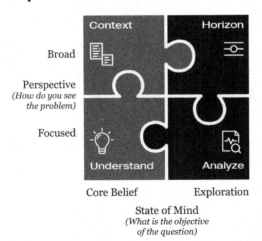

Figure 8: Bradley Blind Spot Map: A = Aim

Aim: Covering the Understand Quadrant in the Bradley Blind Spot Map

Aim is all about being purposeful. Many people feel it's enough to say, "Let me throw a budget at analytics and see what comes out." I don't recommend that model. You need to have an idea in mind that holds value at its core. This doesn't mean that you can't, at any time, change your direction or even your plan. It also doesn't mean that where you've initially chosen to end up is where you'll land. What it does do is provide you with a frame of reference, a starting point to begin the process of discovering your Blind Spots.

Let's look at the bottom-left quadrant of Figure 8.

Tapping into the power of Aim, your first goal is to ask questions that seek to establish Context. To do this, start with a Core Belief, or something that you that you believe to be true.

There are three fundamental questions that will give you a good sense of how to Understand your challenges and/or opportunities and create Context. Start in the bottom-left box in Figure 8 and ask yourself the following three questions:

1. What are your challenges and/or opportunities?
2. Why are they important?
3. What would have to be true for this to be correct?

Feel free to ask additional questions, but these three questions I've found to be very helpful, especially the third one, which is likely the most important.

Let's start with an example question to show how to navigate the bottom-left quadrant of the Bradley Blind Spot Map using Aim. During my work on rolling out DSL for the state of California, the first question I asked myself was, "What's my biggest challenge or opportunity?" The challenge was improving our Mean Time to Repair, a common metric technology companies use to measure the length of time it takes for a problem to be fixed. My question was "How do we improve Mean Time to Repair?"

My second question then was, "Why is it important?" It was important because customers will switch services if we didn't keep our commitment.

Then I asked, "What would have to be true for this to be correct?" Well, there must be viable alternatives in the marketplace. We must be able to meet our commitments to our customers. We need a system that accurately allows us to be able to project if we can meet that commitment before we make it, and so on.

Aim: Couering the Contert Quadrant in the Bradley Blind Spot Map

We'll use Aim to tackle the Context quadrant of the Bradley Blind Spot Map. This box expands on the Core Question you asked in the Understand quadrant to consider its Context. It's a way to put things in a Broad Perspective.

Let's look at the top-left quadrant of Figure 8.

To create Context, ask questions that get at three basic areas: value, location, and identity. To understand value, the best single question I have found to ask is simply, *what's the benefit of answering my Core Question?* Think about how you and your organization benefit from asking your Core Question. For example, the benefit to asking how to shorten customer lines in a retail store is time savings. Your goal here is to take a Broad Perspective.

To Understand location, ask how a change in the environment impacts your Core Question. Location may or may not have an impact, but your goal should be to take a Broad Perspective. A good question to start with here would be, *Does my Core Question have the same level of importance in all locations where we operate?* Feel free to ask other questions along these lines.

The final question in the Context quadrant targets identity. Identity specifically asks, *does my Core Question apply to my customers, partners, suppliers, and so on?* Your goal here is to have a discussion to ensure that your primary stakeholders are impacted the most. A great question to ask to stimulate this thinking is, *how are each of your stakeholders impacted by your Core Question?*

Now, let's go back to the example question: How do we improve the Mean Time to Repair?

Value: *What's the benefit of answering my Core Question?* Customers value their time above all else. The core value here is time.

Location: *Does my Core Question have the same level of importance in all locations in which we operate?* Sure it does. After discussion, we believe customers in every area we serve value their time.

Identity: *How are each of my stakeholders impacted by my Core Question?* The customer experiences significant impact, since they paid for a service that's not working. Partners may be concerned with how this service outage impacts their business reputations. They may be blamed for the service outage when they were not the cause. The supplier will be concerned about their capacity to deliver within the stated Mean Time to Repair. Any changes you make to improve your commitment could increase their cost. After discussion, we maintained that our original stakeholder, the customer, is impacted the most and therefore is the correct primary stakeholder.

So far, we have used Aim to take our initial question and find Understanding by taking a Focused Perspective. What was our Core belief? Then, we took a step back to take a Broad Perspective to understand the Context of our question. Now, it's time to move onto Surprise.

Surprise: Covering the Horizon Quadrant in the Bradley Blind Spot Map

Surprise is the second phase of ASK (Figure 9). Surprise is about taking a Broad Perspective—the opposite of the Focused Perspective you took from your current Core Belief. The Surprise this generates encourages you to think about the Horizon of other possible outcomes.

Using the ASK Framework to Navigate your Bradley Blind Spot Map S=Surprise

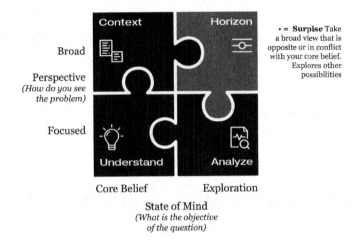

Figure 9: The Bradley Blind Spot Map: S = Surprise

Fundamentally, the Surprise step offers the opportunity to challenge your assumptions to uncover another, more impactful solution that you have not considered before.

Start with the three core sources of value in the digital age:

1. *Cost Value.* You can reduce cost and be seen as a low-cost provider, such as Walmart.

2. *Experiential Value.* You can focus on improving the customer experience. A great example of this is the Chicago-based startup Trunk Club that was bought by Nordstrom in 2014. Instead of the hassle of finding your clothes and outfits in a store on your own, a personal designer/shopper does everything for you.

3. *Platform Value.* You can focus on attracting value through greater interaction with your customer base. Facebook and Twitter are great examples of this. Your platform value increases exponentially the more people interact with your organization or product.

Let's apply these sources of value to our example question: How do we improve the Mean Time to Repair?

In the case of Mean Time to Repair, we wanted to save time. Here, the priority was cost value. The Surprise step flips that assumption on its head. The question to ask would be, "What if our customers don't care about time?" or more specifically, "What if customers don't care about Mean Time to Repair?" Or, if you delved deeper, you might ask, "What if Mean Time to Repair isn't even the most significant use of the customer's time?" That's a great Surprise question because it forces you to pause and reconsider your Perspective as you get closer to that *aha!* moment.

Kindle: Covering the Analyze Quadrant in the Bradley Blind Spot Map

The final step in ASK is Kindle. But what does Kindle mean? We've asked the Horizon question above to see other possibilities. Now, we come full circle to determine if the Surprise question or our original Core Question is the most high-value question to ask (Figure 10).

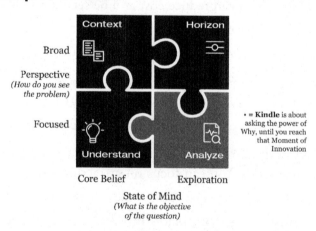

Using the ASK Framework to Navigate your Bradley Blind Spot Map K=Kindle

Figure 10: The Bradley Blind Spot Map: K = Kindle

The first question in Kindle is straightforward: do any of our answers imply that we may be asking the wrong question(s)? In our example, we started with the assumption that Mean Time to Repair was the most important element because customers value how important their time is. Our Surprise question uncovered that Mean Time to Repair may not be the most significant use of customer time in their experience working with us. That sounds like we could potentially be asking the wrong Core Question.

If you feel that you have indeed been asking the wrong Core Question, it's time to Analyze and uncover our Blind Spot. The questions you ask to Kindle understanding of your true Core Question are called *Why-Why-How*. If you get through *Why-Why-How*, you'll uncover whether you need to come up with a better Core Question that will enable you to have high-value answers. In our example, we have determined the Mean Time to Repair wasn't the key issue. *Why-Why-How* will help us uncover the Core Question we need to discover the key issue.

Why: *Why is the problem a symptom of a greater issue?* It could be because customers had experienced greater inconvenience when the service went down in the first place.

Why: *Why is knowing this valuable?* It would mean that Mean Time to Repair is simply about damage control. The problem—the customer down-time—has already occurred. Customers didn't care how long it took to fix the problem. They only cared that their service wasn't working.

How: *How can we change the question to reach a high-value answer?* We could ask, "How do we improve the product so it doesn't break down in the first place?"

Whoa! That's what we should have been asking. We had found our Blind Spot and arrived at our *aha!* moment.

My team and I had spent months developing the right answer to the wrong Core Question. Ultimately, the Core Questions that we should have been asking were, "How do we stop customers from leaving," and, "How do we improve the product so it doesn't break in the first place?" While our customers truly did value their time, the most pressing challenge was that it broke in the first place.

As we went through the ASK process and reached our *aha!* moment, we began to understand that while we had great improvement around Mean Time to Repair, our customers were still leaving us. What about our process was failing us?

This path of inquiry then led us to create an entirely different tracking mechanism that we called installation reports. Here, we began to analyze how many incidences occurred, how many problems occurred immediately following the initial installation, within thirty days of the installation, and then, eventually, within seven days of installation.

Where Do You Go from Here?

Hopefully, you now have a good understanding of the importance of identifying your Blind Spots. The Bradley Blind Spot Map compares your Perspective—Broad or Focused—versus your State of Mind. Are you coming from a standpoint of a Core Belief or do you tend to come from a standpoint of Exploration? Were you more comfortable being free from any type of Core Beliefs, and starting from a clean slate? Those two forces combined allow most of us to capture and see where we are, where we tend to be, and what the other elements make up our Blind Spots.

Next, we'll discuss how to improve your listening skills to create better questions and drive high-value answers. More specifically, what questions should you be asking about in the digital age, and how can you leverage the Questioneering ASK technique to ensure that you apply it in a way that allows you to build sustainable advantage? I call this sustainable advantage the *Convergence Edge*. Let's dive into it in the next chapter.

CHAPTER SIX

The Convergence Edge

SO FAR, WE'VE DISCUSSED *how* to ask the right, high-value question. But equally important is developing the knowledge to know *what* to ask about. One of the best ways to become a great Questioneer is to first become a great listener. Specifically, you need to tune into the ongoing key feelings, behaviors, and constant market transitions in our digital age. It may overwhelm you at times. Let's be honest—with more than twenty million devices and their constant streams of information connected on any given day, it's difficult to know *what* to prioritize. To interpret the data and divine the important actions you should be taking as a result is extremely difficult. And just what are all these devices, text messages, notifications, and settings doing? Essentially they're *pushing* answers at you. It's very easy to slip into the Answer Mindset.

Living in the digital age is a lot like playing a continuous game of Jeopardy, where coming up with high-value questions is imperative to your success. Questioneering is about regularly choosing the *best high-value questions* to ask daily and then exploring the answers that are embedded deeply throughout your entire value chain, from product or service creation to customer acquisition. Additionally, you must define the critical areas you should be listening to as you seek to create better questions. We'll talk about this process more in later chapters.

A Lesson in Listening for the Digital Age

With the power of the internet and social media platforms such as Facebook and Twitter, news travels faster than ever before. Businesses must deal immediately with the emotional reaction to information they release into the mainstream. When this data causes a negative public reaction, remaining silent is no longer an option.

Simultaneously, people say they're continuously experiencing sensory overload from being constantly connected, especially in times of crises. This information onslaught ultimately causes an inability to understand the important factors converging in today's world. In fact, many people just stop listening.

Listening to the effect data has on your business's reputation, combined with the ability to comprehend the *emotional* state of your customers, and further, understanding the drivers of *momentum*, are three factors converging in the digital age. As a business leader, you must consider these three factors simultaneously when conducting business. Let me explain what I mean by this through a real business crisis.

In June 2015, Apple announced the launch of Apple Music, a new streaming music service that would allow customers to download music, stream, and listen to their favorite radio stations all in one application. It also promised the streaming service would learn your musical tastes and preferences and make recommendations for new songs based on your listening patterns. It sounded like a great idea.

As part of the launch, Apple gave their customers a three-month free trial as a means of incentivizing them to sign up to the service. During this time, Apple announced it woudn't pay royalties to the musicians whose music appeared on the site. Taylor Swift, the American singer-songwriter who had quickly become a leading contemporary recording artist, publicly disagreed with this approach. Over social media, she asked how Apple could possibly think they didn't have to pay her for the use of her music, and presume to do so without asking her—the artist's—permission.

On a Sunday morning, Swift posted a stern but professional request on Tumblr: "We don't ask you for free iPhones. Please don't ask us to provide you with our music for no compensation."[10] Her 60 million followers heard her message and were ready to support her request.

Consider the gravity of what was going on here from an Apple executive's perspective. All of a sudden, 60 million people, plus the rest of Swift's fan base, hear that Apple is refusing to pay artists their royalties. By Sunday evening, Apple had responded. They understood this wasn't simply a question of not paying royalties. The high-value question—what Swift was really talking about—was, *What's the value of music in a digital age?*

How soon would it take you to respond if someone posted a negative comment online about work that you've done, or about you personally? Would you even be in tune enough to have spotted the comment in the first place? Let me share how a Fortune 100 company would react.

First, leadership would schedule a meeting to brainstorm who should be involved in crafting the response. Then, they would call another meeting to brief those individuals directly involved in the situation, followed by another meeting where those individuals would provide their input.

Then, yet *another* meeting would be scheduled with the people who would take this input and consolidate it into a single response. Several more meetings—with legal, with the marketing department, with IT, and so on—would be scheduled before a response statement was issued.

If this sounds unrealistic, I can assure you this happens in many companies around the world. Hence, the reason why so many organizations don't respond to a customer complaint at all, or when they do respond, it's too late. The damage has been done.

So, how did Apple respond?

You've got to give them credit. Apple was immediately aware of the post and the enormity of the situation it posed. Specifically, they were aware of the *data*, that Swift was an artist with a tremendous following—60 million people and counting on social media—that gave her a great deal of influence. Apple also understood the strong emotional element behind Swift's complaint. She didn't make her statement via a formal letter to Apple's legal team, but rather appealed to the common *emotion* of fairness, representing all artists who struggle to make it, only to have some large corporation, a David and Goliath-type entity, if you will, take advantage of their creative work.

This direct emotional appeal energized people. I think that Apple also understood the power and impact of *momentum*. In this digital age, information and opinions spread instantaneously. As a result, reputations can be improved or destroyed in a matter of seconds. Both good and bad news can spread like wildfire from the power of momentum. Millions of people were tuned in to Swift's comments and would instantly form an opinion of Apple based on how the company chose to respond. Consequently, their response would have a dramatic impact on the valuation of the company.

Apple's response was brilliant. Ultimately, one of the most powerful companies in the world agreed to the demands of a twenty-five-year-old pop star. They said they would pay the royalties. But *how* they did this is what's really important. Apple's statement, posted on Twitter, read: *We hear you @taylorswift13 and indie artists. Love, Apple.*[11]

Apple not only understood the impact of the data in the form of Taylor's powerful public admonishment. They understood the importance of responding quickly. Additionally, they understood that it was important to respond empathetically.

"We hear you" is a very personalized response. It says, "We understand. We sympathize. We got your message. We took it seriously. We hear you as an individual." They then signed off, "Love, Apple." Again, another personal, emotional appeal that demonstrated their commitment to one of their top-selling artists. Instead of calling Swift or sending her attorney a letter, Apple chose to respond via a platform that could build momentum. They understood this platform could create a positive momentum around Apple and around what they were ultimately trying to achieve with their response, which was to say that Apple recognizes the value of music in a digital age and that there's a place for artists to create value in that digital age.

The Rule of Three to the Rescue

Data. Emotion. Momentum. These factors played a large role in both Swift's message and Apples response to it. Together, they make up the Rule of Three, as applied to business today. When you combine three things that occur simultaneously, they contribute to a more value-centric whole.

The Rule of Three has been the foundation of various subjects, including:

1. *Music*: (three-note triads form the building blocks of harmony).
2. *Religion*: The concept of the triple deity or Holy Trinity.
3. *Drama*: Aristotle's three unities: time, place, and action, or the three-act structure.
4. *Comedy*: Set-up, anticipation, and punch line.

The Rule of Three is also prevalent in business. Steve Jobs was a master of this technique. He applied it to nearly every presentation and product launch he oversaw for Apple.

In 2007, when he introduced the first iPhone as the third of Apple's revolutionary product categories, the first two being the Macintosh laptop and the iMac. Jobs slowly repeated the names of the three products until the audience finally figured out he wasn't talking about three separate devices, but rather one device capable of handling tasks from all three devices.

Then in 2010, when he introduced the first iPad, Jobs used a slideshow that portrayed the new tablet as the third device between a smartphone and a laptop. The tablet itself came in three models: sixteen, thirty-two, and sixty-four gigabits of flash storage. When he introduced the iPad 2, he differentiated it from the first version by highlighting the fact that it was thinner, lighter, and faster than the original.

The Rule of Three is prevalent throughout almost everything we do. It helps us break complex ideas down into smaller parts so we can more easily understand them and then take responsive, agile action as needed. The good news is you can continuously use the Rule of Three to your advantage in the digital age.

Introducing the Convergence Edge and LIKE System

The Rule of Three's factors—data, emotion, and momentum—combine to create what I term the *Convergence Edge*. All three of these factors converge in the digital age (Figure 11). They will help you form a significant knowledge base to powerfully apply the principles of Questioneering. Used effectively together, they'll drive unprecedented results in this age. But to be effective, you'll need practice a systematic approach to listening.

Convergence Edge

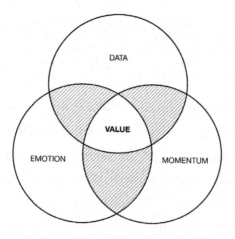

Figure 11: The Convergence Edge

Given all the noise and all the answers that bombard us every day, it's important that you have a listening process you can follow for fifteen to thirty minutes every day that will help you open up to listening and thus to the impact of these three important factors. This will allow you to form a stronger base to continue to ask high-value questions that will yield better answers and build value.

For this purpose, I've created the LIKE listening system:

Listening

Infrastructure

Knowledge

Engagement

Listening today requires you to open your mind and senses to the digital world all around you. Effective listening also involves being purposeful. An effective listening Infrastructure starts with a successful process—a way of going about listening to attain maximum value. You develop Knowledge by not judging whether what you heard is right or wrong, or if you agree or disagree, but rather by seeking to understand and comprehend the value of the what you're hearing. Engagement involves responding quickly and empathetically.

In the chapters ahead, I'll share with you more details to help you learn and master the LIKE system. Your goal should be to apply the elements of LIKE for fifteen to thirty minutes each day until you develop a strong ability to listen effectively. Let's apply LIKE to the beginning of our listening journey with the first circle of the Convergence Edge: data.

CHAPTER SEVEN

Learning to Listen When Data Talks

Data. The world is overwhelmed by it. In fact, in 2017, 90 percent of all data had been generated over two years, 2015 and 2016. And it's still growing. By the end of 2020, 1.7 megabits of new information will be created every second for every human being on the planet. Market intelligence provider International Data Corporation (IDC) predicts the big data and business analytics market will hit $203 billion by the year 2020, up from approximately $130 billion in 2016.[12]

What does this mean for leaders? It means we'll have a heck of a lot of pressure on us to take all the answers the daily barrage of data provides us and act upon them. The concept that data equals answers is at the core of what data means in a digital age. Unfortunately, it also means people stop listening. We're bombarded by an overwhelming number of answers, which causes us to shut ourselves off from questioning. As a result, we constantly grab quick answers and act upon them, taking little or no time for reflection, discernment, exploration, or any other form of vetting. This is the trap of the Answer Mindset.

Since data is so plentiful, most of us also take it for granted. We don't *leverage* it to more effectively address the challenges or opportunities we face daily. I can't wait until I get more emails in my Gmail box. I can't wait until my refrigerator is so connected that it's sending me messages that I'm out of milk. I can't wait until my car is telling me everything that's going on with it, sending more emails and more text messages. Obviously, I'm joking. Few executives would say to you, "Hey, what you need to do is send me more data."

The overwhelming amount of data being sent our way makes it increasingly difficult to benefit from the data onslaught. So, most of us don't use any of it. That's not a sustainable solution. Think about the last decision you made. Whose advice did you listen to that helped you make your decision? Most people come up with two or three sources. You might have even included yourself, having tapped into your own gut intuition. You might also have listed a favorite individual on your team who sees eye-to-eye with you. You sought out that person knowing the two of you share a common perspective. We don't tend to talk to detractors. That requires too much energy and effort. Finally, you might have included a data source, such as an ERP report or a white paper.

The drawback to this approach is that for you to be able to ask good questions, you must be aware of the Blind Spots in your listening infrastructure. As I mentioned in the last chapter, you discover your Blind Spots by developing a process for listening.

With a firm awareness of what's happening in the digital world (nurtured by the ASK system—Aim, Surprise, and Kindle), you can build and optimize a strong, constantly growing knowledge base. But without a solid listening infrastructure, the chances of aligning yourself to the right target by continually asking high-value questions, and therefore finding the high-value answer, are greatly diminished.

Last chapter, I introduced the LIKE listening system: Listening, Infrastructure, Knowledge, Engagement. This process allows you to leverage data, emotion, and momentum—the factors that contribute to the Convergence

Edge—to improve your knowledge base and ask high-value questions. Let's take a look at how.

Listening and Learning with LIKE

You can apply the LIKE framework to the first core factor in the Convergence Edge: data (Table 1).

**LISTENING INFRASTRUCTURE
KNOWLEDGE ENGAGEMENT**

**Listen For The Impact Of Data On
Your Business Environment**

	Descriptive *What happened?*	Diagnostic *Why it happened?*	Predictive *What will happen?*	Prescriptive *What should be done as a result?*
Internal Sales ERP System	# of Units Sold			
Customer Verbatims		Products / Services not user friendly		
Weather Report			Storms in the east, causing delays in shipping	
NY Times - Amazon				Storms in the east, causing delays in shipping

Table 1: LIKE Listening System for Data

The first column lists your potential listening sources. The row across the top indicates four fundamental types of data and how to listen for them:

73

1. *Descriptive*. What happened?
2. *Diagnostic*. Why it happened?
3. *Predictive*. What will happen?
4. *Prescriptive*. What should be done as a result?

Let's start with the top row. Descriptive data provide answers and valuable insights into the question, *What happened?* Descriptive data typically reveal insights from the past. Listen to your data sources to understand what happened. What is Descriptive data showing you through their patterns?

As a business leader, you might listen for the average weekly sales data or weekly revenue volume data. Or, as a manufacturer, you may listen for how many units you produced last week. A service business leader may listen for the number of customer calls their employees have taken. Each Descriptive data listening source provides you with a better sense of what happened inside your organization over a certain period of time.

The next type of data to listen for is Diagnostic data. Diagnostic data provide answers and valuable insights into the question, *Why did it happen?* Like Descriptive data, Diagnostic data reveal insights from the past.

Often, Diagnostic listening sources are verbatim. Customer feedback is a source of Diagnostic data. They may tell you they were upset because of X or Y. This feedback provides you with the *why*.

The third type of data is Predictive data. This type of data helps you answer the question, *What's likely to happen?* The patterns in Predictive data help you make an educated, informed guess at what may occur.

Predictive listening sources answer questions such as "What's going to happen?" or "What will likely occur?" A good example of a Predictive listening source is your favorite meteorologist. Meteorologists are in the Predictive data business. "Next week, I believe there's a likely chance of rain, or maybe a thunderstorm or some strong winds," one may predict. These weather experts listen to Predictive data sources to give them a sense of what will happen in the near future.

Finally, we have Prescriptive data. Prescriptive data provide answers to the question, *What should I do as a result?* Prescriptive data contain insights into what actions may occur as a result of the findings of your data.

Prescriptive data listening sources provide answers to questions about what people may choose to do based on a belief they hold about the future. In other words, if it's going to rain, a Prescriptive data listening source may say, "Wow, we project that we're going to increase production in umbrellas."

With any of your listening sources, your goal is to listen to understand what's going to happen, why it's happening, what will happen, and ultimately, what should be done about it.

Your Gut Feeling Is Not Enough

Now, let's turn our attention to the left column, your data listening sources (Table 1). List your data sources down the column. Once you have your list, you can now begin to fill in the table. Match them with type of information the data delivers so the answer for your Descriptive data question corresponds to your Descriptive data listening source, Diagnostic data to Diagnostic source, and so on.

I challenge you to stretch your thinking in terms of how much perspective your listening sources can provide you. You might have a preconceived belief or problem on your mind. Your first goal is gain clarity and understanding of this problem. This requires you to think beyond your gut and look to your Descriptive, Diagnostic, Predictive, and Prescriptive listening sources.

You might say, "My gut is telling me we need to accelerate our sales by adding more features to the product." Why? "Because I've seen it before many, many times," you may reply, or perhaps a customer recommended the change. At this point, you have to fight the urge to give into the Answer Mindset and ask yourself why do you believe this to be true. Let's assume it will take at least ninety days to implement any solution you come to. Isn't it worth spending one hour thinking about the sources you should listen to over the next few days to inform your decision?

What report can you commit to reading or listening to every morning? What experts on Twitter, Tumblr, LinkedIn, or other social media platforms make good listening sources for you? What about the detractors in your organization, the people who never seem to think the way you do? How are you listening to them and where does their input fall? Are they describing what happened? Why it happened? What will happen?

Are you considering the macroeconomic or economic indicators of what you're observing? Are you listening to community and social data? What about information about what your competitors are doing? The list can go on and on, depending on your position in your organization or your current position in life.

The important thing to bear in mind is that listening isn't solely about the end destination, but the journey. You'll gain tremendous value in identifying data sources and discovering data insights, whether or not these insights directly answer your initial question. The point is to improve your rate of learning.

And as your rate of learning accelerates, so too will your ability to drive high-value questions with the ASK Process, as the breadth of your knowledge also increases. As you grow proficient with using your listening infrastructure, the disjointedness of the information flow will lead you to follow the ASK process and ask high-value questions.

For example, what if your preconceived belief was that to increase revenues, you needed to add additional product features. I strongly believe the core source of value for your customers is feature addition. But what if the data show the majority of your customers use only a small set of the total available features? Then using the ASK Process, you may uncover your Surprise question, *What if customers don't value depth of functionality as the main product differentiator?* In other words, what if enhancing the experience associated with a core set of features is far more valuable than adding additional ones?

Exercise: Establish Your Daily Data Listening Routine

Lastly, I'd like to share how you can create a daily process for listening more effectively.

Every morning, pick five listening sources and write down what you observed from listening to them. Ask questions such as:

1. Are my observations telling me what happened?
2. Why did this happen?
3. When it will happen?
4. Are they telling me what people have done?

Take fifteen to thirty minutes every day to write down what you've observed from tapping into your listening sources. This will expand your art of the possible and improve your ability to ask high-value questions.

When you tap into the power of these questions using the ASK Process, you'll have a greater awareness of the data that the digital age, with its constant barrage of answers, is providing you. Use the LIKE format to generate more questions that will challenge your current assumptions, helping you drive breakthrough innovations.

Soon, you expand what I call your Horizon of Observations. You'll realize deeper and a more concise set of observations that can help you more quickly achieve your goals. Note that this process is just the first element of the full circle.

Finding Data Listening Sources

For many, the prospect of carving precious time out of your day to analyze data may seem daunting—and of little value. "I'm not a data scientist," you might say. "I don't have the resources or the ability to possibly analyze all this information. And besides, it falls outside of my business. It's not something that my business has resources for, so how do I even get access to this great data?"

The key to building a great listening infrastructure for data is your ability to connect to resources outside of your organization's four walls and your core network. You need the ability to dynamically engage and disengage knowledge. So, how do you do this?

First, identify readily available resources. Multiple sites provide access to data in non-traditional ways. Kaggle is a data science community that allows you to pose different questions about your data to the group. Perhaps you found a data set that you think is interesting. Or maybe, as you're listening, you find some economic indicators that have you asking, "Wow, I wonder what these mean? I wonder if these indicators have any tie to our ability to drive revenue?" These are great questions. You can post it on Kaggle for very little expense. Upwork is another great site with thousands of individuals who can assist you with analyzing information. Some charge as little as $10 an hour to help you analyze critical data patterns.

Tapping these resources can help you answer questions very quickly, but they can also help you understand and improve your data listening skills. You just need to know where to look.

Second, you need to expand your data listening beyond the data you have in your organization. For example, McKinsey did a great piece of analysis on the value of open, or free, data. Open-source data is valued somewhere between $3.2 billion to $5.3 billion. For the most part, the government generates this kind of data. The bottom line is that this data is available for your use for free. Additionally, it's constantly updated.

However you gather your listening sources, make it a daily priority to improve your listening. Apply the LIKE infrastructure to improve your listening for data sources. Consider the four categories of data that we've discussed: Descriptive, Diagnostic, Predictive, and Prescriptive. Use Table 1 to tap into your listening sources when you're thinking about or solving a problem. Fifteen to thirty minutes first thing in the morning is all the time you'll need.

As you begin to do practice listening to data, you'll become increasingly aware of the variety of answers that will emerge. You'll then begin to see how important it is to fundamentally hone your skill at asking high-value questions.

But data is only one factor of the Convergence Edge. Consider the Apple story from the last chapter and how they handled Taylor Swift's call-out online. Remember that the "E" in LIKE stands for *Engagement*. Engagement is important because it allows us to interact with others and create an emotional connection. Emotion is the next element we'll focus on. It'll help you answer the question you're most likely asking, *How do I identify and create an emotional connection with my customers?*

CHAPTER EIGHT

Stay in Tune with Emotion

I HAPPEN TO TRAVEL a great deal. In fact, I often travel 300,000 miles in a year. Inevitably, at least once a year, I'll walk into an airport and suffer the same panic attack: I'll reach down and find that I don't have my Bose noise-canceling headphones. Why is that a problem?

It's a problem because as I'm sitting in the airport at my gate, this lovely young couple appears with two well-behaved kids, ages two and four. All is calm and quiet as they give their tickets to the attendant and board the plane. However, as they look for their seats, something changes in these well-behaved kids. Their only mission suddenly becomes to find me—Joseph Bradley—no matter if I'm in the front, middle, or back of the plane, first class or economy. It doesn't matter. Those two kids will find me, and when they do, they'll share their great excitement to be on this trip with me by kicking and shaking my seat and making as much noise as possible to let me know they're there and that they're truly excited to be on this plane.

And that's why, when I see those well-behaved kids at the gate, I reach down in search of my Bose noise-canceling headphones. In the moment I realize I don't have them, this Joseph Bradley isn't the same Joseph Bradley looking for a pair of headphones on the weekend. My emotional state in each scenario is distinctly different. At the airport, I don't care what a new pair of headphones costs. All I care about is getting my hands on them. I'll rush to the airport kiosk, and maybe I'll buy one or two pairs. I just want to make sure I get those Bose headphones.

It's important to note that Bose airport kiosks are close to the gates. Someone thought of stocking the display with items most travelers would find critically important. Someone also designed the kiosk so the buying experience is as seamless as possible so I can get on my flight without delay. These were both strategic decisions that created a strong, positive response on my part as an impulse buyer in a hurry.

And that other Joseph Bradley, who's not at the airport? That Joseph Bradley strolls into a Best Buy store on the weekend. He wants to engage in intellectual conversation about decibel levels and the noise-canceling characteristics of these headphones. This Joseph Bradley wants an experience.

Before the digital age, business leaders would see the airport Joseph Bradley and the Best Buy Joseph Bradley as the same buyer. In the digital age, this is no longer true. Two distinctly different buying patterns with two distinctly different motivations can exist in a single buyer. As a marketer, a business leader, a product manager, a customer support specialist, and finally, a human being in the digital age, we need to understand how to connect with and capture value from the emotional state of customers best provide and create higher value. We have to be in tune with the emotional state of our customers.

The Power of Emotion

Most companies measure whether their offerings appeal to their customers based on customer satisfaction. That's been the measurement for years. While customer satisfaction is certainly one measurement, it only gives you a general idea of whether value is being created for the customer. We're much more sophisticated in the digital age.

For you *Star Wars* fans out there, think of the lightsaber used by all the best Jedi knights and compare it to the blasters used by the Storm Troopers. The lightsaber is the sophisticated weapon of choice, as Obi-Wan Kenobi in *Star Wars: A New Hope* states: "Your father's lightsaber. This is the weapon of a Jedi knight. Not as clumsy or random as a blaster. An elegant weapon, for a more civilized age."[13]

In the real world, what's the more "elegant weapon" to improve the customer experience? As we've advanced into the digital age, so too has our ability to move beyond just merely tracking whether a customer is satisfied or not. We can tap into context to assess what's happening with and around them to get a sense of their emotional state.

The *Harvard Business Review* released a study that found emotionally connected customers are 52 percent more valuable on average than those who are merely highly satisfied. Emotionally connected customers are deeply invested in the product or service being offered.

We can open ourselves up to listening to the data—the information coming from our action—we then can listen to and understand our customers' emotional states and intents. This is far more valuable than asking customers whether everything has been done to their level of satisfaction or simply guessing.

The Birth of Digital Humanism

Earlier in my career, I had the opportunity to build a solid relationship with the former CEO of our company. My role at the time was to assist the CEO in articulating our value proposition to our customers, targeted specifically at their senior-most leadership. Our CEO believed our current strategy was cemented in our legacy business and would cause us to be blind to upcoming market transitions. His challenge to me was a simple question that had powerful implications: "What's next?"

It's always extremely difficult to describe a future that has not occurred.

But that wasn't the high-value question I needed to answer. The high-value question was, *how am I going to convince the most talented resources in our company to work extra hours on a non- customer billable project, when they're already at their max on customer work?*

In other words, how was I going to create an emotional connection with a select group of employees to work on a project without revealing that the ask was from our CEO? Not revealing the ask was critical because our CEO didn't want his position to influence the result.

I identified a core group of five team members and enticed them to dedicate time to discuss a future when an unparalleled explosion in connected devices digitized the physical world. As you can imagine, it was a slow process. First, I listened to the team's comments to determine their emotional level. Initially, many jokes were made about how this work would engineer everyone out of jobs. But then, it became evident many people felt we *were* proving a case for how machine would take over our jobs. It certainly didn't help that we had just gone through a forced reduction in the past quarter. The basic emotion of self-preservation and survival generated a great deal of energy, debate, and most importantly, questioning. All of a sudden, my struggles shifted from how to get people to respond quickly to calendar invites for our meetings, to what restaurant can deliver food past 10 o'clock in the evening. The team had grown emotionally connected to the project and didn't want to stop working.

When I reflect on this now, I see that because I opened myself up to listening more consistently, I became much more aware of the emotional concerns of my fellow co-workers. I was better able to entice them to still dedicate their time to work on this project.

Suddenly, what had started out as a simple inquiry of what was next, evolved into me giving a presentation to our company's board about the IoE. The board asked why I felt this was so important. I reflected for a moment and responded, "You know, there are two core reasons."

It was at this moment that I came up with the notion of Digital Humanism. I continued, "Everyone in the world right now is talking about the IoT replacing people. Machines *are* going to replace people. If you truly believe this, however, you're missing the boat.

If you go down that road, you're undercutting your potential for success. It's not about merely reducing costs as a means of improving your bottom line. Sure, it's a solution, but it's a very short-term solution. It's a right answer, to a wrong question. The true power and value of the IoE is in enhancing the ability and the power of people to create and innovate new things that we didn't even think were possible. It's to be a *multiplier* of the power of the human spirit. That's the power of the IoE."

Think for a moment about the Marvel Comics hero Iron Man. Iron Man didn't replace a person. No, Iron Man was who he was because of the superpowered suit he put on. In the suit, he can run faster than ever before, use his enormous strength to beat up bad guys, and tap into his amazing vision to see things that are not otherwise visible. Iron Man took what was human and simply made it better. That's the power of the IoE.

When I came back in the office, several of my team members said, "Joseph, you were so right. We've got to ensure that people, that the enterprise, that CEOs and leaders understand that this is the power of the IoE." It wasn't about replacing people. It was about using the power of the human spirit and magnifying that strength with technology. That was what was so motivating.

At the time, I didn't understand the depth of the importance of this concept, but what I had done was open myself up to listening, gathering, and understanding the importance of emotion and the various touchpoints held by all stakeholders involved. And by listening and being in tune with the emotional elements of this problem, I was able to get my colleagues excited and generate energy about working on this project. It blossomed into one of the greatest pieces of analysis that has ever been done. We soon renamed the IoT the IoE.

Get in Touch with Your Customers

If you're tuned into the emotional touchpoints of your customers and other stakeholders, you'll find yourself regularly inspired. Now you'll be able to leverage a more powerful means of not only asking better, high-value questions, but driving the best high-value answers to those questions. As we have highlighted previously, it's not about the end destination but the journey. It's critical that you establish a starting point upon which to begin listening for the emotions of your customers.

Historically, science has recognized six core emotions: happy, sad, afraid, surprised, angry, and disgusted. However, in 2014, the Institute of Neuroscience and Psychology published research stating that the distinction between four of these emotions was based on social interactions and constructs. Instead, they said, human emotion is based on four core emotions: happy, sad, afraid/surprised, and angry/disgusted.

As a business leader, you want to listen for the drivers of these emotions, the emotional motivators. Hundreds of emotional motivators drive consumer behavior. A 2016 study in the *Harvard Business Review* focused on how an emotional connection matters more than customer satisfaction. In the analysis, authors Alan Zorfas and Daniel Leemon identified ten emotional motivators that significantly affected customer value across all categories studied.[14] I've taken these ten and focused on the top five that apply to the customer experience.

These five emotional motivators include the desire to:

1. Stand Out from the crowd, to be known as someone unique.
2. Feel Good, a sense of well being.
3. Feel a Sense of Thrill, an overwhelming experience.
4. Be Responsible to our environment and society.
5. Feel Safe and Secure, to know what you have today will be there tomorrow.

Now, let's take a look at Table 2.

LISTENING INFRASTRUCTURE KNOWLEDGE ENGAGEMENT

Listen For The Emotional Motivators Of Your Customers

	Uniqueness *Stand out from the crowd*	Feels Good *Sense of well being*	Thrill *Overwhelming experience*	Responsible *Good for the environment*	Trust *Safe and secure*
Social Hubs	Customized Cell Phone Covers Trending				
Social Hubs		Rolex Watch Associated With Success			
Social Hubs			Men over 40+ purchasing Augmented Reality games		
Social Hubs				Re-usable bags trending on Instagram	
Social Hubs					Comments on Apple Facial Recognition

Table 2: LIKE Listening System for Emotion

The five emotional motivators are in the top row of the listening infrastructure. Your listening sources are listed down the first column. What are these sources telling you about the emotions of your customers. How can these results be interpreted? Are you missing data for certain emotions? Is this because you need to listen harder, or is there a shift of emotion happening in a new direction? Remember, all things can be important, but not all listening sources are equal.

If you realize the sources you're listening to are not giving you the emotional connections you want, you may need to look for more socially-motivated listening sources—sources focused on social responsibility. A Google search of the term "socially responsible" returns millions of results. Find experts talking about the things that are important to you. Follow more of these experts. Open your listening sources so that you can start to grasp the emotional motivators that are driving your customers.

The hardest part of using the LIKE method is committing yourself to the time it takes to first find and then set up your listening sources. Certainly, the pure number of data sources being identified and the exponential growth in those sources is a challenge.

We've talked about the Convergence Edge and listening to data and emotion. Now, let's discuss the third factor of the Convergence Edge and complete the Rule of Three for the digital age: momentum.

CHAPTER NINE

Leverage Momentum

KICKSTARTER IS PROBABLY ONE of the most significant disruptors of the last fifty years in terms of how businesses can get funded. On the site, individuals invest in products or services by pre-buying them without receiving and equity. In an effective campaign, the amount of funding a project or company receives is directly proportional to customer uptake. If done well, people will invest merely on the promise to deliver a product or service. Individual provide funding, but more importantly, they become customers.

One of the first companies successfully funded on Kickstarter was Bragi. Developed in 2012 by the Danish entrepreneur Nikolaj Hviid, Bragi's product, Dash, is the holy grail of wireless headphones. They not only play music, but also provide a Siri-like function in your ear.

How would a budding entrepreneur get funding for a product like Dash? Think about the pre-investment required to generate this type of technology and get it into the marketplace. Through Kickstarter alone, Hviid raised $3.4 million. Today, Dash is now well on its way to selling 600,000 units a year. [15]

Another great success story from Kickstarter is Dwarven Forge, a company that builds miniature gaming terrains. Founder Stefan Pokorny is an avid gamer and artist who creates live terrains for gamers that feature incredible detail. You can only imagine the costs involved in creating all the miniature hand-painted pieces, figurines, and other interactive elements.

Pokorny launched a Kickstarter campaign that specifically targeted the gaming community. Remember, on Kickstarter, the customer doesn't receive any ownership of the company in which they invest. What they do receive are the bragging rights to being among the first to say, "I'm one of the first to have this product." Dwarven Forge raised $8.2 million in four separate Kickstarter campaigns.[16]

The power of the momentum of buyers on Kickstarter and the ability of entrepreneurs and other individuals to leverage that momentum is truly incredible. More than 14 million backers invest in projects on Kickstarter. Most are regular people who have decided to be among the first to gain a piece of a particular product. Hundreds of thousands of products have been funded in this way.

The challenge with working with a venture capitalist firm is that while you're asking for money, they're asking you tough questions about the viability of your product or service. Venture capitalists want proof that your product is already being adopted in the marketplace before they'll give you the cash. If you persuade them you have a viable investment in exchange for their financial support, they expect you to give up a significant portion of your company.

Kickstarter figured out the answer to a high-value question many would-be entrepreneurs ask: "How can I build support for my product and, at the same time, fund my business?"

Leveraging Momentum

Business leaders used to have three main sources of leverage: time, energy, and money. Time is obvious. It's the time that you spend leading your organization or yourself in the workplace. Next, energy helps you stay positive. You dedicate and assert your energy to making sure that things move forward in a positive way. Finally, you leverage money as you continue to invest in your products and services. But then along came the digital age, and many leaders found a virtual rug had been pulled out from under them. Leaders today must approach business from an entirely new mindset.

We've already talked about the need to leverage data. To be effective, you must connect with your customers on an emotional level. As a result, emotion is your second source of leverage.

The third source of leverage is momentum. Momentum is widely overlooked when we think about one's ability to listen, create, and drive value today. You leverage momentum to quickly generate an exponentially increasing amount of support for an idea, product, service, or belief. You can leverage momentum by asking for money to invest in a particular project. But you could also develop a persuasive presentation that gains the hearts and minds of your end users. So, how can you blend those two ideas into one action?

Gaining Traction

Your ability to identify strong new product or service offerings by listening to and engaging with your potential customers will generate the momentum you need to improve the rate of product or service adoption and traction in the marketplace. This is about harnessing the enthusiasm of your potential customers. It won't cost you a dime, as it generates its own energy. That's the power of momentum.

In a non-business context, 2017 witnessed one of the most amazing and overdue movements in the world: the #MeToo Movement. It called for women to be treated as equals in the work environment based on their merits and their ability to create value for a corporation and not be subjected to harassment and discriminatory practices and behaviors. Because of momentum, #MeToo gained traction throughout the world. It was even awarded *Time* magazine's Person of the Year in 2017. This is yet another vivid example of the importance of momentum in the digital age.

But for something—anything—to gain momentum, you must have your listening infrastructure in place and in tune to the world around you, whether you're getting funding for a product or service on Kickstarter or raising awareness about discrimination against women in the workplace.

Imagine not being aware of what's going on around you or having any sense of listening. Imagine not knowing the types of questions you should be asking in a particular environment or situation. This shows you the power and importance of creating and maintaining an open listening infrastructure in your organization and your personal life, too.

It isn't enough to just be concerned about end results. The end will never justify the means because without listening first, you'll never know if the end is the one you should be striving for in the first place. Even the greatest achievements the world has ever seen might not have realized their full potential because their creators weren't listening for or truly appreciating the value of the talent available to their organizations at the time of the breakthroughs.

There's no question that momentum is critically important to successful Questioneering. So is the ability to draw from vast amount of resources to best apply high-questions to ensure you're not implementing the right answers to the wrong questions.

Applying the LIKE Listening System to Momentum

When applying LIKE to momentum, there are three critically important drivers you need to listen for (Table 3). Feel free to add more drivers as you go along, but the three I'm about to highlight should be your foundation.

LISTENING INFRASTRUCTURE
KNOWLEDGE ENGAGEMENT
Listen For Drivers Of Momentum

	The Crowd	Collaboration	Community
Kickstarter	Conversational AI – gathering significant investment on crowd sourcing platforms		
Medium, Twitter		#MeToo being discussed across multiple platforms	
LinkedIN Groups			Google employees upset over what they perceive against female engineers

Table 3: LIKE Listening System for Momentum

The first driver is Crowd. The Crowd is a group of people who individually contribute to achieve a similar goal, but aren't working together or interacting with each other. They also aren't looking for a sense of community. Their motivation is purely transactional.

Uber is a great example of the Crowd. Think about the impact it has had on transportation. Its success lies in its ability to leverage people's appreciation its adeptness at providing transportation affordably, reliably, and quickly. Similarly, as discussed above, the people who invest on Kickstarter do so because they value the transaction. They want the end product.

The second driver of momentum is Collaboration. This occurs when a group of people work together to achieve a shared goal. These people interact, help one another, and generally make a greater contribution to the project they're focused on.

Collaborators still desire a transactional value, but primarily, they want to improve how they use a particular platform and how they derive value working with others. They don't necessarily want a sense of community, but they do want to improve the use of the platform.

A terrific example of this is the website Medium. Medium users improve the platform by posting compelling questions and, consequently, soliciting a significant number of opinions from others. The more questions and opinions shared on a platform, the greater the value to users. Its founders say, "Medium taps into the brains of the world's most insightful writers, thinkers, and storytellers to bring you the smartest takes on topics that matter. So whatever your interest, you can always find fresh thinking and unique perspectives."[17] Great stories and social interaction drives value through Collaboration.

The third driver is Community. Here, a group of people interact with one another to enhance their sense of belonging and shared identity. Folks contribute to the group not necessarily to achieve a particular outcome, but to serve the group itself and further a common mission or identity and experience connection. This sense of belonging to a particular community defines the individual's identity. The Community still seeks the transactional value of the Crowd and Collaboration, but it's also looking for that emotional value and, primarily, a sense of belonging.

Consider all the various discussion groups on LinkedIn. These groups are created solely for building a sense of community, of making people feel they're not alone and that there are others out there who are experiencing the same or similar challenges. From this shared sense of community and experience, participants learn from each other and grow together. Crowd,

Collaboration, and Community are the three building blocks of momentum. As you gather your momentum listening sources, ask yourself if each listening source:

1. Fits with my overall plan, or am I just listening to this for pure transactional value?
2. Lends itself to the Crowd?
3. Lends itself to Collaboration?
4. Lends itself to Community?

My point is simple: if you want to understand how to build momentum, you have to be aware of what is driving that momentum today. Therefore, make sure you're paying attention to a listening source in each of the three driver of momentum.

Finally, listen actively. Capture what each of your listening sources says. If you have been listening to your Crowd sources, you would have uncovered years ago that the ability to share assets or services between private individuals, either free or for a fee, has been building momentum for years. Whether in performing household duties, sharing bikes and automobiles, or homeowners renting out rooms and entire homes, this phenomenon has been building momentum. What questions do you think traditional hotels asked themselves that prevented them from asking the high-value questions Airbnb founders Brian Chesky, Nathan Blecharczyk, and Joe Gebbia asked? As of January 2018, Airbnb was valued well over $30 billion, more than Hilton Hotels.[18] This is just one of many examples why listening to what's building momentum in the Crowd is critically important.

The same can be said for both Collaboration and Community. The inability for companies to identify problems in their product or services that begin to build momentum in Collaboration platforms can be devastating. Imagine the impact of not listening to the ideas of and saying no to the contributions of 51 percent of your workforce! Yet that's exactly what has happened in the US because we were not actively listening to what women have saying for years. The impact of #MeToo is far too great and important to even think of quantifying. I can only imagine what we could have achieved if we would have only listened.

Returning to the ASK Process

We now return to the ASK process with a whole new level of insight. Now that you've created listening infrastructures for data, emotion, and momentum, reflect on how your starting point would be different when you begin with Aim. Imagine your improved ability to use the element of Surprise based on your newfound listening infrastructure. And finally, imagine your ability to really Kindle high-value questions. Now you've truly expanded your knowledge.

I encourage you to use the listening infrastructures we've covered in the last three chapters at least fifteen minutes a day. Focus on your data listening in the morning and emotion at lunch, once you've gotten a chance to get into your day. Round out your afternoon with momentum.

These exercises will increase your breadth of knowledge, giving you a richer frame of reference for creating the high-value questions that deliver high-value answers.

In Section III, we'll look at some real-life situations many of us experience every day. We'll apply the ASK process and the Convergence Edge to give you a practical way to ensure you're asking high-value questions to discover high-value answers.

CHAPTER TEN

Cost Cutting:
Right Answer, Wrong Question

IMAGINE YOU RUN A leading professional services firm that focuses on helping clients implement and gain value from technology. It's your end-of-quarter staff meeting, during which your leadership team discusses the state of your business in that quarter. You start bright and early. You get in the room. You say your hellos. Everyone is upbeat. You anticipate a great session.

But then your finance director shares that while the company was on pace to have a profitable quarter, it ended up missing its revenue target. Not only did the business miss its target, it also missed its margin for the quarter. The finance director goes on to say that what's critically important is getting back on track. Every team *must* make its numbers in the next quarter. Next, the finance director asks the recurring, core question: "How do we cut costs?"

"Oh great, here we go again," you think. "Yet another cost-cutting drill." This happens every year. You know what comes next. Your finance director goes on to say the company needs to think about various cost-cutting initiatives it can implement quickly. Then, the director asks you to schedule a meeting with your team to brainstorm all the ways in which you can reduce costs.

You go back to your team and start brainstorming answers to the all-too-typical question, *How do we cut costs?* You and your team come up with the usual solutions:

1. Institute a hiring freeze.
2. Limit travel to customer-facing meetings.
3. End all internal travel.
4. Eliminate contract spending by cutting back on the use of contractors.
5. Cut any costs related to innovation or noncustomer billing activities.

Then, you turn your focus to employee perks and giveaways. You stop the free sodas in the cafeteria. You delay promotions and possibly freeze or cut any type of employee recognition programs. You continue down the list of usual suspects on the chopping block.

Now, you think you've got a strategy. You go back into the group meeting with your peers and your boss asks everyone to read off their recommendations and ideas. Of course, while you're presenting your list, you want to make sure that you include the proper risks associated with those ideas. You say, "Hey, we should stop hiring." But if you stop hiring, you run the risk of losing revenue or facing a decline in customer satisfaction. So, you go around the room and hear your peers' suggestions and the risks associated with them. Unsurprisingly, they're all very similar to yours.

Next, the group prioritizes the actions you'll all take to reduce costs, but you realize you can't prioritize anything or make any decisions because there are too many risks to consider. You and your peers are told to go back to your teams and give it some more thought. The meeting ends.

A week or two later, you get the email. All problems have been solved. The previous meetings where you tried to determine where to reduce cost by weighing critical versus non-critical programs have been pushed aside. With the simple stroke of a key, the Excel guru in your organization has solved the problem. Leadership has decided to make cuts across the board.

Every team gets their fair share, regardless of business risk or performance. Everyone has great reasons why their part of the business is critical and should not be reduced. But you've been given a number to meet, plain and simple. You immediately start putting into effect several of these initiatives to meet your cost-cutting number.

Sadly, the above scenario goes on across multiple organizations on multiple continents regularly. When you hear the question, "How do we cut costs?" everyone relives the same playbook. You act as if there will be a breakthrough innovation, but in reality, everyone assumes their usual roles and executes the usual, comfortable answers, all of which, time and again, result in the same low-value outcomes.

But what would the above scenario look like if you used Questioneering? The process would prompt your company's leaders to ask a better question, *How much time did we spend on asking if reducing costs is the right high-value question?* Zero. Instead, the finance director asked a question that put you into the Answer Mindset. You assumed the usual roles while simultaneously going through the usual motions of making the same number of cuts you've made year in and year out. Remember the definition of insanity: Doing the same thing over and over again, but expecting different results. Let us use Questioneering to stop the insanity brought on by the answer mentality.

Implementing Questioneering

Let's track our progress so far. We've spent a great deal of time on how to arrive at asking high-value questions using the ASK process: Aim, Surprise, and Kindle. We've also discussed how to improve your listening skills so you can apply the Surprise and Kindle elements of ASK more effectively.

Additionally, we've built our listening infrastructure through the LIKE listening system, based on building your Listening, Infrastructure, Knowledge, and Engagement around data, emotion, and momentum. These two elements of Questioneering help you understand how to ask high-value questions. Now, we'll bring these concepts even more closely together so you can apply your new Questioneering skills to a real business challenge, *How do I cut costs?*

Before we begin, understand that by asking this question, you align your entire focus on cutting costs. Everything about the organization, everything you discuss with your team, centers around the question of cutting costs.

Start by applying the ASK process. Begin with Aim (Figure 12), which is all about getting clearly focused. Ask yourself and your team:

1. What is our initial objective?
2. What are our Core Beliefs?
3. What are our challenges or opportunities we want to accomplish?

Your initial objective is to cut costs to improve your financial position. You believe this will allow you to meet your objectives for the quarter, which must improve over last quarter.

Using the ASK Framework to Navigate your Bradley Blind Spot Map A=Aim

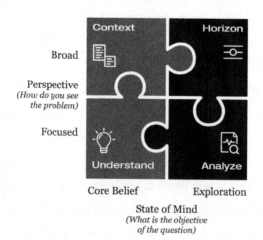

Figure 12: The Bradley Blind Spot Map: A = Aim

So, what would have to be true for this to be correct? Why must you improve your performance over last quarter? You'd have to believe your quarter numbers must improve for your investors to be happy. You'd also have to believe you can't grow your topline or influence revenues within the quarter. In addition, you would have to believe cost cutting, which seems like a low-hanging-fruit strategy, will affect performance this quarter. And finally, you also have to believe Wall Street values current this quarter's performance more than the future direction of your company. Therefore, it's critical you meet your current quarter goals. This is your Core Belief.

When applied to the Bradley Blind Spot Map, this Core Belief is very Focused. You're starting in the lower-left quadrant of the map. The next step of the ASK process is to consider a Broad Perspective to better understand Context.

To do so, you ask your team, "Is our Core Belief relevant to every team in our organization?" You agree that fundamentally it is, since you believe cost cutting is important across your organization. You discover that while the broader organization missed its numbers, your particular team actually hit its revenue target. And because your team hit its target, it also made its operating margin. But since you're looking at the company as a whole, your team still has to make an effort to reduce costs. You know leadership will include everybody in the exercise of cost reduction, so from a contextual standpoint, it's important to understand that while you've made your numbers, you're still part of a broader organization.

To build a greater understanding of context, you ask your team, "What do we believe is the core source of value behind our Core Belief?" Ultimately, your core source of value is expense savings. You believe cutting expenses is a cost-saving exercise that will help you meet your goals for the quarter. Why? When you really think about it, the underlying Core Belief is that you cannot control revenue during the quarter, but you can control costs. You also have the Core Belief that everyone must participate in cutting expense or risk not being seen as part of the team. But the most important Core Belief you have at this point is that your problem is isolated to just this quarter. You've never had this problem before, so it's a one-time problem, right?

Challenge What You Believe to Be True

Now you've now gone through the first element of the ASK process, Aim, and you're clear about the problem you're solving and your Core Beliefs. Now let's shift to Surprise, the second step in the ASK process of Questioneering (Figure 13).

Using the ASK Framework to Navigate your Bradley Blind Spot Map S=Surprise

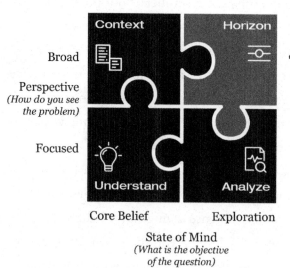

Figure 13: The Bradley Blind Spot Map: S = Surprise

The Surprise step is when you challenge some of your current Core Beliefs. As you do, employ the LIKE listening system. Start with Listening questions to uncover potential data listening sources, such as, "How do we draw upon our existing information to understand what question(s) we should be asking?"

One listening source may be the stories of other companies. In Amazon's first several years, it lost money. But because Wall Street believed in Amazon's recurring revenue business model, they traded at a higher multiple, and Wall Street rewarded them. Investors believed the future performance of the company held more value than its quarterly performance. By listening to data and learning how it's being applied in the digital age, you're better able to ask high-value questions.

Below are some questions, based on the LIKE listening system, that may reveal you're asking the wrong question. Do any of these give us a hint that there might be high-value questions you should be asking instead?

1. What would have to be done for us to drive profitability in the quarter?
2. What if we can't control costs in the quarter?
3. What if most of our costs are fixed?
4. What if we *can* control revenue, and that's actually a Core Belief?
5. What if this problem isn't related to the current quarter, but is systemic to how we conduct our business? In other words, what if this problem isn't isolated to just this quarter? An *aha!* moment!
6. What if meeting our current objectives for the quarter isn't the main source of value? What if Wall Street rewards future potential over existing performance? Another *aha!* moment!

Let's focus on the fifth question, one of the *aha!* moments, as we move to the third step in the ASK process, Kindle (Figure 14).

Using the ASK Framework to Navigate your Bradley Blind Spot Map K=Kindle

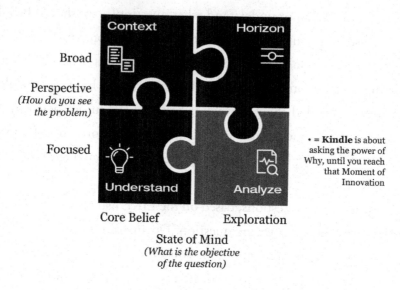

Figure 14: The Bradley Blind Spot Map: K = Kindle

Once you ask, "What if this is systemic?" you turn your attention to internal data. You review past employee satisfaction surveys—an excellent emotion listening source—and discover many employees have feelings of fear or insecurity. Employees have endured cost-cutting exercises every quarter. They have been fearful for their jobs. They also have been fearful of sharing new ideas and innovating. This very important listening point directly supports the notion that your problem isn't isolated merely to one particular quarter.

Allow me to interrupt our exercise for a moment. I hope you've just had a real-life *aha!* moment. Believe it or not, many organizations around the world currently treat cost-cutting as if it's simply a one-time quarterly event. But if you were to ask for and listen to feedback from employees, it becomes explicitly clear that cost-cutting isn't something that only happens once a year, but a constantly recurring issue.

Now let's continue the ASK process for your Surprise question. What would have to be true for the problem to be systemic to how you conduct your business rather than isolated within a particular quarter? The first thing you'd have to believe is that the way you capture value from existing services causes you to fall behind. Something is broken, and it's causing this problem to occur over and over again. *Aha!*

Kindle Why: Why Is Cost Cutting a Symptom of a Greater Issue?

At this point, it may be valuable for you to explore this *aha!* moment further at the Surprise step of the ASK process. But let's finish our exercise and move on to the last step, Kindle, so we can uncover your Blind Spot. It's time to apply *Why-Why-How* to the new, high-value question we've uncovered, *Why is the way you're capturing value today causing you to fall further and further behind in the market?*

Let's return to our initial objective: to cut costs and thus improve quarterly performance. Why do we need to keep cutting costs? A possible answer may be, "Since we price our services based on the number of hours it takes to deliver a solution, we're constantly having to sell new services every quarter." But what if you realized companies are moving to pricing models that are *not* based on the amount of hours it takes to deliver a solution? Rather, these new pricing models are based on the value their solutions deliver to customers on a recurring basis. Could the perceived need to cut costs be a symptom of this greater issue?

By shifting the conversation to how much value customers receive from your solutions, it moves the conversation away from how many human hours it took to create the solution. As an example, when you purchase Salesforce, you don't pay an hourly rate based on the time it takes them to install the software. You pay a recurring charge based on its perceived value.

Kindle Why: Why Is Knowing This Valuable?

Why is this valuable? Because of the ability to scale. Now, you're not constrained by having to hire and train new resources every time you generate additional revenue.

But what if you say something like, "In our current model, every time we sell a service we have to balance our available workforce with our new projects. This often results in us accruing added costs to hire and train new employees. Additionally, because we must constantly sell new projects to generate revenue, we have periods where we have too many people with not enough billable work. This really causes us to have a cost problem." Here's your Blind Spot: *Why do we have a cost problem?*

We're getting closer. One more step.

Kindle How: How Can We Change the Question to Reach a High-Value Answer?

The current services you offer requires you to scale up, adding more employees, rather than scaling your intellectual property or software, which doesn't have additional costs. In other words, we need to scale on intellectual property (IP) versus people. Whoa, okay. You just had your *aha!* moment.

We started this conversation having you ask the question, *How do we reduce costs?* But now, you've come up with a better, high-value question, *How do we change our business model to scale on IP versus cutting people?* The second high-value question we came up with is, *How do we shift a greater percentage of our sales to a recurring revenue model?*

Think about those two questions and the answers that are going through your head. You can now ask high-value questions such as, *How can we change our model to scale on IP versus cutting people?* You're thinking about software and micro-services. You're thinking about analytics and partnerships.

Next, compare these new answers to your prior answers around cost reduction. It's clear that in this case, you discovered high-value answers as you followed the ASK process. But the key to following that process is to spend time reflecting more deeply and, from there, asking better questions. If you find yourself asking the same question multiple times, it probably means you were asking a low-value question rather than uncovering the high-value question. What can't be overstated is the importance of how you can shift to asking surprise questions that challenge your Core Beliefs. It's about *fueling* your thinking.

Listening and Learning Fuels Your Thinking

What helped fuel the shift in thinking in the scenario above was taking the time to improve your ability to learn through Questioneering. The process you followed ensured you listened to your data sources to better understand your particular issue. Then, following the ASK process, you were able to take data points that clearly allowed you to identify what happened, why it happened, what will happen, and what actions to take. You understood and listened to the emotional state of your employees and customers. In the exercise, we only identified one emotion listening source: employee satisfaction surveys. We found employees felt fearful and insecure after enduring the cost-cutting process over and over again.

The other critically important factor you should listen for are drivers of momentum. If we had listened to external listening sources of the Crowd, Collaboration, or Community, we probably would have picked up several examples of how value-based pricing and subscription revenue is fundamentally gaining momentum in the marketplace.

Internally, one of the strongest drivers of team momentum is competition. One of the things I'm sure you'll discover is that many people in your organization are driven by competition: "We want to beat competitor X or competitor Y." A statement like this generates energy. Taking advantage of how momentum drives your team helps you ask better high-value questions, such as, "How do we change our business model scaling IP in a manner that builds momentum versus cutting people?" It also helps your team come up with unique, high-value answers.

An Even Better Question

Here's another high-value question: *How you would put yourself out of business?* What this question does is place you on the other side, with your competition. You'll be surprised at the level of energy and momentum this question brings to an organization. I led an organization where every quarter, I talked with employees and gave them insight as to how the business was doing. I'd ask them for feedback after the session and would get maybe a 5 to 10 percent response rate. But then I asked the question, "How would you put us out of business?" Now *that* yielded a dramatically larger response rate!

Also, because I asked that question, employees started to bond, saying things such as, "Hey, we're a part of this company," and "You'll want to listen to me, as I'm going to tell you what you're doing wrong. I'm going to tell you how I'd put you out of business." It was amazing. Our response rate that went from 5 percent of our employees to closer to 55 percent. And they didn't just respond; they wrote a book about it!

I now ask this question every quarter. I can't emphasize enough the importance of actively building your listening infrastructure to better understand your business environment through data, the emotional motivators of your customers and employees, and the core drivers of momentum.

CHAPTER ELEVEN

Create High-Value Answers

AS I MENTIONED EARLIER, I've had the good fortune to do quite a bit of basketball coaching. I've coached both boys and girls at the elementary, middle, and high school levels. Many of the teams I've coached experienced a great deal of success. However, I've never focused on winning championships as a goal.

People have often said to me, "What's your goal? It's gotta be about championships. You gotta win championships." But, I've always considered winning championships not as an input, but an output. In other words, winning championships is the *result* of something, of performing a certain set of activities. If you focus on doing those activities correctly, you should win some championships. Winning is the result of hard work.

When I coached basketball, I focused on builder my players' skills in five areas: defending, rebounding, passing, moving without the ball, and shooting. If my players and I established a strong foundation in these skill sets, we'd win games. And if we won games, we'd win championships. That was my focus in becoming a good coach and building a good team. It's also the same focus I've brought to my career and to how we should attain and leverage high-value answers and subsequent breakthrough innovations.

Driving breakthrough innovations is an outcome, a result. It's the equivalent to winning championships.

Up until now, we've focused primarily on how to generate high-value questions. Questioneering teaches you to create high-value questions that lead to high-value answers, resulting in breakthrough innovation. If there's one thing I want you to take away from this book, it's an understanding of how to ask high-value questions. If you're asking a low-value question, the rest of the process doesn't matter.

Think of Questioneering as a birthday cake. The core part of the cake— the really good stuff—is forming and asking high-value questions. The icing on the cake is all about high-value answers. The icing is important, but it's only 20 percent of the overall value. You've got to get the other 80 percent—the actual cake—right first. So, it's now time for us to talk about that 20 percent: How do you drive high-value answers?

Clarify, Align, Achieve

Once you're certain you're asking the right high-value question, there are three ways to ensure you'll come up with a high-value answer: clarify, align, celebrate.

First, any high-value answer must be clear and consumable. We've all heard reports on how our attention spans are shrinking. In 2015, Microsoft conducted an intriguing study that found the average attention span for a goldfish was nine seconds. In comparison, the study showed that the average person's attention span was eight seconds.[19] And, believe it or not, that number has since *shrunk*!

You read that right: goldfish have a higher attention span than humans do. Our attention spans and patience for learning are shrinking. Therefore, whatever we attempt to share with others must be as clear as possible. We have very little time to grab someone's attention and establish a connection.

Second, you must work quickly to gain alignment within your

organization. This is key. The longer it takes you to gain alignment, the longer it will be before your organization can implement your high-value answer and achieve value. The worst-case scenario is that you never gain alignment. Without alignment, you'll never know if you had the right answer to your high-value question. When different teams of your organization commit to a few elements of an action plan or don't buy in at all, it's impossible to understand if you have landed on a high-value answer.

Imagine designing a play in basketball. How would you know if the play works if only two of the five players on the court run the play? The answer is you wouldn't. It may be a great play, but without all team members executing and committing to the play, there's no way to attain accurate results.

Third, you must achieve success often. Otherwise, you'll never build momentum. Remember, all things can be important, but not equal. There are many competing initiatives and programs in a company. Various action items and possibilities also compete for your attention as an individual or entrepreneur. So how do we, as employees or individuals, ultimately choose what gets our attention? I've found it's all about energy. How much energy do we have to expend, and how much do we get back?

If we put forth a great deal of energy but we don't see success quickly, it becomes increasingly harder to stay focused. You seek out replacements for the things that aren't working. When I say success, I don't mean that you must reach your end goal; rather, I'm referring to measurable progress that provides you with a feeling of accomplishment and inspiration to move forward. This is the momentum that moves you toward success. Just as we've talked about momentum being an important component of your listening infrastructure, momentum is also crucial to driving high-value answers.

Understanding the 1-2-3 Model of Execution

Whether I was driving implementation in the first deployment for high-speed broadband services and DSL in California, creating the strategy for the IoE, or implementing more than two hundred solutions across global Fortune 1,000 companies, time and again, I've used the 1-2-3 Model of Execution to drive to high-value answers:

1. Communicate a clear goal on *one* page.
2. Give yourself *two* weeks to gain alignment from all your stakeholders.
3. Give yourself an additional *three* weeks to achieve your first success.

1-2-3: one page, two weeks to alignment, three weeks to success.

You drive the 1-2-3 Model of Execution with a process I call QBAM: Question, Belief, Action, and Metrics (Figure 15). QBAM is a method of operating that drives communication, alignment, and clear action to improve decision making. In other words, it gets you to breakthrough innovation.

QBAM

A method of operating that drives communication, alignment, and clear action to improve decision making.

Figure 15: QBAM

1. **Question**: Most of this book discusses how to generate high-value questions. Through the ASK process, you identify the question that uncovers the high-value problem or opportunity you or your team have agreed to solve. You need to state clearly what that is.

2. **Belief**: What must be true for the question you're asking to be of high value? Through the ASK process and the Bradley Blind Spot Map, you've come to understand your Core Beliefs. It's very important to state what those Core Beliefs are. It helps you understand the problem you want to solve and why. Core Beliefs also provide you with clear insight to who your key stakeholders are. Key stakeholders are people who have an interest in or direct control over your delivering on your Core Beliefs.

3. **Answers**: These are the one to three key actions you must take to transform each Core Belief into a fact. You can't predict the future, but you can make the future, and these answers should turn those beliefs into facts.

4. **Metrics**: Finally, how will you know when and if you're right? Metrics will tell you.

1: Clarify

Once you've completed the QBAM framework, it's time for the first step in the 1-2-3 Model of Execution. Put the outcome of your QBAM framework on a single page or slide. If you can't succinctly communicate what you're trying to accomplish and how you'll accomplish it, you'll never gain alignment and momentum in your organization. Think of your single page or slide as your elevator pitch. Without it, you'll never gain the clarity or sense of purpose you need to achieve clear alignment.

Have you heard the expression, "Brevity is a Virtue?" It's especially true in business. For your message to gain momentum and be accepted and absorbed across your organization, you must present it as succinctly as possible. Imagine if your metric was longer than one slide or page. No one's going to read it. Think about it.

By definition, momentum is built when others can understand and further your cause, even when you, the owner of the work, are not present. A single page that clearly states your objective and any required details makes it easier to consume for those who will execute your objective without your involvement. When was the last time a colleague gave you an eighty-slide deck and you actually took the time to read through it to understand each element? When's the last time you read your organization's full business plan, absorbed every page, and internalized all essential details? I bet it was a long time ago, if ever.

The environment in which we live and operate doesn't encourage us to sit down and consume detailed content in written form over multiple pages or slides. In fact, I congratulate you for making it this far in this book! You're probably in the minority. Most people these days merely skim through content or read a few highlights here and there, looking for answers. If you're going to effectively communicate and drive the Questioneering process, you've got to keep your message short and to the point. Implement the QBAM framework regularly to achieve effective business decision making and alignment.

I use the terms *Questions, Beliefs, Answers,* and *Metrics* instead of *vision* and *strategy* because you need a vocabulary that's very clear and provides transparent decision making. It cannot be nebulous. If you want to be successful when you go to a meeting with your peer group or in a session, leverage the QBAM framework. Be explicit about the high-value problem or opportunity your team is answering. Spend 80 percent of your time Questioneering to find clarity. Be clear about your Blind Spots, actions, and outcomes before presenting your problem or opportunity to the group. Give people a common vocabulary and the opportunity to be on the same page.

2: Align

Regardless of your position or the industry in which you work, more often than not, the thing that derails a discussion or meeting isn't that people disagree, it's that they're championing different parts of the conversation. In other words, they're each trying to achieve different goals. Someone may be pushing one Belief, while another is pushing a Metric, while someone else is saying you should Answer a different Question or focus on execution. The QBAM framework ensures you and your team are on the same page throughout the discussion. It also provides an excellent framework for conducting productive meetings.

Question, Belief, Answers, and Metrics. Is this a meeting where we're going to focus on Questions or are we going to address the Answers to our Core Beliefs? Is this a meeting where we determine how we'll ultimately know if we're right? It's very important that we know, going into a meeting, what the focus of that meeting is going to be. Another benefit of the QBAM framework is that it serves as a repeatable and transparent process for how we make decisions, how our organization aligns to those decisions, and how we hold ourselves accountable to those decisions.

3. Achieve

Most organizations cannot identify the decisions they've made. They've never documented them. If you were to ask, "What are the top decisions you've made for the year?" they wouldn't be able to tell you. This is a huge problem. The QBAM framework provides you with a one-page framework to understand the answers and the decisions you've made as an organization so you can track whether you've made the right ones or not. The QBAM framework also allows you to track who was involved in making those decisions. Documenting your decision making is tremendously important.

Putting the 1-2-3 Model of Execution to Work

Now let's look at an example of the 1-2-3 Model of Execution at work (Figure 16).

Framework

Q	How do we eliminate in lines in our stores.		
B	Customer value their time as Cart Abandonment drives tremendous loss in revenue.		
	TECHNOLOGY EXIST TO ELIMINATE WAIT TIMES	CUSTOMER WILL ENJOY A CHECKOUT LESS EXPERIENCE	NO LINES CAN BE EXECUTED IN A WAY THAT CONSUMES LESS TIME THEN LINES.
A	1. Predict checkout volumes 2. Leverage Video analytics to predict customer movement and emotional state.	1. Mobile App Checkout designed with 3 clicks or less 2. Mobile App includes help button where on staff personal to assist or remote expert 3. Allow for social experience to share purchases	1. Ratio of staff on hand to customer in line will be 1 to 7 2. Checkout can happen anywhere in the store 3. Detect customer frustration and proactively assist
M	1. poV executed	1. 5% Revenue Increase driven by Cart Abandonment	1. Basket to vehicle time reduced by 20%

Figure 16: QBAM Framework Example

Let's go back to the story I told at the beginning of the book about the store that focused initially on reducing the customer's wait time in line, but then turned to the high-value question, "How do we eliminate lines in our store?"

Let's now use the QBAM framework to answer that high-value question.

As we've already determined our high-value Question, we'll start with our Core Belief. We know customers value their time because when they wait in line, they abandon their carts. What must be true for this to be a Core Belief?

One, for us to believe we can eliminate lines in our store, we must believe technology exists to eliminate wait times. We also must believe customers will enjoy a checkout-less experience. And finally, we must believe eliminating checkout lines consumes less time than customers standing in line. Why did we invent lines in the first place? At least initially, checkout lines were an orderly means of getting people through checkout and out the door with what they needed. We would have to eliminate lines in such a way that reduces time.

Now, let's consider some of Answers. What are the one to three actions under each of these Beliefs that would turn that them into fact? First, let's tackle how we could use technology to eliminate wait times. One, we could predict checkout volume. Two, we could leverage video analytics to predict customer movement. Three, we could use technology to learn the customer's emotional state.

Now, let's turn to the second Belief, that customers will enjoy a checkout-less experience. How can we turn this Belief into a fact? One, design a mobile app that will allow a person to checkout in three clicks or less. Two, include a Help button, where on-staff personnel are summoned to help an individual. Or, the customer could opt to have a remote expert via video right there in the app help them through the checkout process. Third, create a social experience so the customer can share what they're purchasing, get their friends' opinions of it, or whatever the case may be. If we do those three things we will, without a doubt, turn that Core Belief into a fact. We'll create a reality where customers enjoy a checkout-less experience.

What about the question of whether eliminating lines consumes less time than having lines? Think about the shopping experience in an Apple store, where you can seamlessly learn and engage with a product or expert before you make your purchase. The process of finding a product and figuring out if it's the one you want doesn't need to be extended by the checkout line process. We can combine this into one seamless experience.

So, what actions can we take to make this belief a reality? We could have a 1:7 ratio of staff to customers. For every seven customers potentially ready to check out, we'll have one staff person on hand. We'll also make it possible to have a pleasant and expedient checkout experience anywhere in the store. This is critical to ensuring a faster checkout experience.

We also need to detect customer frustration and proactively assist the customer before they reach the emotional state that damages their experience and compels them to abandon their carts. We believe these answers will in turn create an environment where each of the Beliefs we've laid out will translate into fact.

Then how do we know we're right? With the technology that exists to eliminate wait times, we'll execute a proof of value (Figure 16). We'll measure whether our proof of value will be a success. Our Metric is whether we can do a proof of value and show that technology works.

Second, customers will enjoy a checkout-less experience. We'll measure the reduction in cart abandonment. If fewer customers abandon their carts, then we should see an improvement in revenue of approximately 5 percent. Therefore, our Metric is a 5 percent improvement in our revenue driven by cart abandonment. We'll also reduce the basket-to-vehicle time, the time it takes a person to put something in their basket to the time they get in their car. We'll reduce that by 20 percent. That's how we'll know the no-line concept is better than customers waiting in line.

What Gets Measured Gets Done

This is a good example of how the QBAM framework works in real practice. But what happens if you can't measure your high-value answer? The truth is, you must believe everything in this world has some subjective or objective evidence against which you can measure success. Admitting you can't measure your high-value answer is saying you don't know if you're right. It's another way of saying you don't have a high-value answer. Sometimes, you may not be able to draw the exact cause and effect.

Questioneers are not attorneys trying to prove a case in a court of law. But it's critically important that we understand what we're trying to achieve and have a proxy for that success. How much that proxy is the contributing factor is up for debate, but you can't have a high-value answer without having a clear way to measure it. The point of the measurement is to drive momentum. Fundamentally, you'll find that you won't be able to gain alignment around stakeholders, and that it would be very difficult for people to rally behind you and gain momentum without an understanding of success. Metrics are critically important in establishing your ability to show success and drive momentum.

So, how do you go about aligning stakeholders in two weeks? Stakeholders are key to executing your high-value answers. You must include them. Typically, the hardest part of gaining stakeholder alignment is showing that your high-value answers are truly valuable. This is the hardest part of the equation because, again, people don't spend any time thinking about whether or not they're creating a high-value question.

The way to ensure and gain stakeholder alignment inside of two weeks is by aligning your high-value answer to what you would have to believe to be true. The stakeholders who own those Core Beliefs are whom you seek to gain alignment with. Many of us make the mistake of believing that you gain alignment in the meeting where you're present and explain your plan.

This is so far from the truth. Gaining alignment isn't an event. It's a process. This process has to be sustained when you're not in the meeting and the key stakeholder is explaining your plan to others, that is, her team. The ability for that stakeholder to comprehend and explain your plan on a single page removes the friction in maintaining alignment as your high-value answer is implemented in the organization.

Aligning your high-value answers to the Beliefs required to be turned into facts ultimately allows you to quickly align stakeholders. That's the magic. That's what allows these stakeholders to take these Beliefs to their teams without you being there to articulate the value of your high-value answers.

QBAM drives you to clear and consumable Answers that ensure you have speed of alignment and Metrics to celebrate success often, so that you can drive and build momentum. This closes the loop around Questioneering. We spent 80 percent of the discussion talking about high-value questions and then 20 percent creating high-value answers, which ultimately drive the breakthrough innovation.

I devote the final section of this book to four questions I believe every business leader, entrepreneur, or individual living in the digital age should have on their list of high-value questions.

FOUR HIGH-VALUE QUESTIONS

CHAPTER TWELVE

What Do I Say When Silence Is Not an Option?

JUST AS DATA, EMOTION, and momentum intersect at the Convergence Edge, the intersection of social, business, and political spheres often forces companies to enter into what has historically been considered a no-fly zone around hot-button social and political issues. But as the competition for technology talent intensifies as we accelerate further into the digital age, silence is no longer an option for businesses.

By 2020, millennials and Generation Z will dominate the US workforce. Generation Z will constitute 40 percent of all US consumers, and they're one of the most connected, socially and politically aware groups out there.[20] They're self-educated, socially conscious, and concerned about the values of the company they work for. By buying products that are sustainable and environmentally conscious, younger consumers are already reshaping corporations' direction. Both groups will reshape the employment landscape with their convictions and the expectation that employers demonstrate similar convictions. One study found 62 percent of millennials are willing to take a pay cut to work for a responsible company, versus the US average of 56 percent.[21] The tech industry, which tends to be purpose-driven, is already heavy with millennials and will also be a draw for Generation Z.

Think about how businesses reacted to President Donald Trump's comment about white nationalist protests in Charlottesville: "You... also had some very fine people on both sides." Leaders from Intel, Merck, and Under Armour all objected to the comment. That kind of response is exactly what we'll see as companies hire upcoming generations and establish a values-driven culture with a strong sense of purpose, so they can land the best of the best.[22]

To maintain a workforce that will carry them into the future, companies will simply have to listen to their employee base and apply their corporate principles to social and political activities. They can't stay silent any longer. In the past, it may have been enough for companies to simply try to stay out of the spotlight during difficult times—if they could successfully avoid taking a stand on controversial issues, they could do their best to ensure that no large section of their customers or key demographics would react badly. But this type of thinking is, more often than not, a result of fear—fear of not being able to find the right solution and therefore running away from the problem. Or instead, a result of seeing other companies attempt to make social statements with their advertising and watching it backfire dramatically on social media.

Two Case Studies: Pepsi and Dodge

Pepsi and Dodge are two examples of major ad programming gone badly wrong due to the reactions of millennials and Generation Z. Take a close look at these examples, because they deserve careful consideration. However, as you're reading about them, don't only think about what these companies may have done wrong in the eyes of their customers, think about high-value questioning: what do these experiences tell us about what companies in the future can do *right*?

In early 2017, Pepsi ran a commercial with model, reality television star, and social media celebrity Kendall Jenner in the midst of a photo shoot.

Outside, there appears to be a protest march in the street. It's hard to tell exactly what the nature of this protest is: it could just as easily be a parade, with hundreds of beautiful, diverse, happy marchers holding generic signs and a few handsome, unarmed police officers lining the street. Jenner sees the activity and decides to leave her photo shoot to join and lead the... march? Protest? Parade? She opens a can of Pepsi and shares it with a grinning young officer, to cheers from the crowd. Clearly, Pepsi is attempting some sort of statement. But what? And how would it be received?

The reaction, mostly online, was swift and decisive. Clearly, Pepsi was trying to make some sort of commentary on political divisions within the country, and to let Pepsi play a starring role in a touching scene of unity, with opposite sides coming together. But the ad was roundly critiqued from almost every side, for its timing, for its tastelessness, and for its trivialization of a powerful moment in societal movements for the sake of making a buck on a soft drink.

The advertisement was strikingly reminiscent of Coca-Cola's famous and very successful 1971 advertisement, the Hilltop ad, also known by the chorus the young people in it sang: "I'd like to buy the world a Coke." The ad came across as a message of hope and unity, of something beautiful that could be created by bringing people together to "sing in perfect harmony." The Hilltop ad became one of the most well-known and beloved ads in America at the time, cementing Coca-Cola's status as a global household brand. What could have made that advertisement so successful, while Pepsi's was such a failure?[23]

The problem appears to have been a severe misreading of the cultural attitudes surrounding protest at that moment in the United States. In 1971, young people responded to conflicts such as the Vietnam War with music and messages of unity. Crucial to the Coca-Cola ad, however, is that they were projecting a message of hope and unity that was powerful because of the nature of the hope it relayed. It didn't claim its music put an end to violence, but brought people together from all over the world to rise up in song. All it did was make the viewer think that it was *possible*. It didn't claim to be the solution; it made its viewers think that *they* could be.

The Pepsi ad, on the other hand, tapped into a dramatically different cultural moment. Let's unpack the reasons it didn't work. The primary reason involves the conversation Pepsi was trying to be a part of. In the years and months leading up to the ad campaign, marches and political activism had taken a new place in American society. Months earlier, the largest, most well-attended march in American history was the Women's March in Washington, DC. Even more significantly, Black Lives Matter protests and backlash against police violence had become a major cultural touchstone in the time leading up to the release of the ad. But the major forces and significance behind these protests movements came from the fact that society and politics didn't appear to have arrived at a solution. Protests don't continue to happen because they're fun, as much as Pepsi made their protest look like a party. Nor do they continue to take place because they have been effective. People in America, especially young people, continue to march because the problems they were protesting had not been solved. It isn't that Americans wanted protests to stop, it's that they wanted them to *work*. Pepsi's ad, which makes a protest look like a celebration and the problem of police violence appear solved by cracking open a Pepsi with a cop, came across not only as ineffective, but as offensive. People felt it made light of the hardship they were enduring just to make money on soda, not to help them in their cause for change.

It wasn't long before Pepsi took down their ad, going so far as to apologize for it, and issuing the following statement: "Pepsi was trying to project a global a message of unity, peace and understanding. Clearly, we missed the mark, and we apologize. We didn't intend to make light of any serious issue...."[24] Pepsi tried to be reactive, and to make its voice part of a movement, but it failed. It appears the failure has acted as a warning sign to other businesses about the dangers of speaking up.

Let's examine another case where a company has gotten hit with backlash for trying to market to a social movement. The Super Bowl is one of the brightest advertising spotlights in the world. Advertising during the Super Bowl holds a unique place in American culture, and ads are specifically tailored for that moment, with the knowledge that they'll be watched, re-watched, and discussed by millions of Americans. Companies often go to great lengths to be noticed during these ads, competing for attention on the one evening every advertiser wants to be the one people are talking about.

The auto manufacturer Dodge chose to use the moment to link their product with an icon from the US Civil Rights Movement. Their ad showed footage of a diverse group of Americans engaged in a variety of types of work—studying, teaching, working construction—and driving Dodge trucks. All of this footage of Americans doing American things would have been fairly generic, if not for the audio playing in the background: excerpts from a sermon delivered by Dr. Martin Luther King Jr., fifty years ago.

Dodge was clearly also trying to engage with a social moment. The ad aired on February 4, 2018, at the very beginning of Black History Month and the forty-year anniversary of Dr. King's sermon.[25] Dodge hoped the words of a civil rights icon would on some level engage with the discourse playing out in American society. The car company associated itself with Dr. King's message of unity to heal the divides characterizing American society in the age of Trump.

The backlash against the Dodge ad was almost instantaneous, airing as it did during one of the most-watched events of the year. Criticism came from several angles. Many perceived Dodge's juxtaposition of Dr. King's remarks with the racial conversation centered around the NFL at the time as a shameless attempt, again, to co-opt a powerful message to make a profit.

The immediate reactions pointed out the irony of using a civil rights icon in a commercial during the NFL's biggest moment of the year. The NFL had a rough year leading up to Super Bowl LII in regard to conversations about race. Colin Kaepernick, a black quarterback, ignited a movement and commensurate controversy by kneeling during the national anthem in protest of police violence. He was targeted by the league, and even by the president, for failing to honor the nation and the flag, Meanwhile, he was defended by supporters and critics of the NFL, who maintained he was targeted for his race and that the league and the president were using racial signifiers in their criticism of a black athlete. With race at the center of conversation about the NFL and its place in society, using a speech by Dr. King was anything but a safe move.

Beyond the social and athletic context of the advertisement, detractors were outraged as well by the selection of Dr. King's words. By combining the audio of his sermon with a truck advertisement, Dodge were naturally trying to cause their viewers to associate Dr. King's message of peace, community, and social support with their brand. This was a mischaracterization not only of Dr. King's broader message, but even the specific speech that they chose. In the very same sermon from which Dodge selected about a minute of audio, Dr. King railed against the idea of advertising itself, going as far as to *single out* auto manufacturers: "This instinct explains why we are so often taken by advertisers.... they have a way of saying things to you that kind of gets you into buying. I got to drive this car because it's something about this car that makes my car a little better than my neighbor's car.... I am sad to say that the nation in which we live is the supreme culprit."[26]

That irony was apparently lost on Dodge, but it certainly wasn't lost on people who responded angrily against the ad. Not only had Dodge taken Dr. King's words and used them to try to sell trucks, but they had done it during a sporting event characterized by racial controversy. To add insult to injury, with apparently no sense of irony, they took words from a sermon in which he criticized the very concept of advertising.

What can we learn from these case studies? Consider again the value of the questions you ask. The experiences these companies had after airing their advertisements may come across as warning signs, but they need not dissuade companies from entering the conversation. They reveal something very important about the people watching these ads: people *want* to engage in difficult conversations and the *want* to feel as though they're achieving a social good.

Where these ads failed was by trying to tell people that they didn't need to make change, that things were fine. As long as you're drinking Pepsi and driving a Dodge, you don't need to act, because our products are unifying elements. Of course, that isn't true. And the people watching the advertisements were smart enough to know it. They wanted to engage—the very fact that they reacted so strongly tells us that. Don't tell people they don't need to do anything. Help them do it!

The fear companies might experience when they see backlash is the answer to a low-value question, "What might the consequences be if I speak out on an issue?" This is the wrong kind of thinking, which is guaranteed to produce unproductive answers. Instead, companies should learn from Pepsi and Dodge's mistakes not by asking themselves how they can use a particular movement but how they can contribute to a movement that aligns with their Core Beliefs.

Consumers and Corporate Social Responsibility

With the expansion of American and global markets, consumers are faced with an incredible range of choices when it comes to choosing a product. It's essential not only to be able to appeal to millennials and Generation Z and make products that are attractive to them, but also to understand what their motivations are.

Millennials and Generation Z are able to research companies with ease never before possible and resources that don't just show them the face companies want to display, but the realities of how companies really act. In 1971, you would be sitting in your living room and you would see a commercial for Coke, with young happy people singing, and this would play a significant part of forming your impression not just of the product, but of the company as well. Consumers saw what companies decided to show them.

The current world of advertising and corporate behavior in the digital age is significantly different. A consumer might be sitting on the train on the way to work, watching videos on the internet, when they see an ad for an iPhone. No doubt, it's a brilliantly engineered ad, showing the viewer everything that Apple wants them to see, in a beautiful pitch that was focus-grouped for reactions and tailored for that particular viewer at that particular time.

These are powerful tools in the modern advertising environment, but they're not enough. Before that person's commute is even over, after they've watched whatever video or read whatever article that piqued their interest, they might be thinking about the ad they saw. Maybe their old laptop is dying, and they're considering buying a new one, so that Apple ad was perfectly timed. With that advertisement fresh in their mind, still sitting on the train, minutes later, they decide to do a little bit of research because, on their handheld device, they easily can. This is the game-changing moment— when the consumer decides to go beyond what a company has decided to show them and look beyond its face with their own research. At this point, Apple can't easily control what the consumer is able to find out about the company. There's an enormous body of reporting work about every major company's behavior available out there.

Within minutes of having seen an ad, a consumer can look into whatever they're most concerned about regarding both the product and company practices. It's possible the consumer just wants to know about the reliability of a computer's battery life or the benefits of a solid state hard drive. But it's just as possible, and increasingly likely, that the consumer is interested in the working conditions in manufacturing plants. Perhaps they're concerned about a company's carbon footprint. Maybe they want to learn more about the diversity of a company's workforce, their sexual harassment policy, the political contributions they make and the candidates they support, the CEO's salary, their relationship with law enforcement when it comes to privacy and data protection—the list goes on and on. It's limited only by the consciousness of the consumer.

A company's profile is no longer just the product they sell and the face they display to the public. In this new era, their behavior as a company in its totality becomes an inherent part of consumers' impression and understandings. And the consumers, especially millennials, really do care. Let's take a look at the numbers.

Association with a Cause

Millennials—the generation born between the early 1980s and the late 1990s—are far more concerned about the behavior of corporations than the generations before them were. More than nine in ten millennials would switch brands to one associated with a cause they care about (91 percent versus 85 percent, US average).[27] Think back to the experiences of Pepsi and Dodge. Millennials don't expect companies to simply acknowledge a cause exists and make bland statements about their values, they expect companies to really *engage* with a cause and trying to further that cause, not just coopt it. To do this, companies must make inroads into the political arena and not worry about being associated with political causes.

Let's examine a case study in advertising that went all-in on political associations. A podcast isn't a medium that tends to make big headlines, but nevertheless this medium's growth is rapid and remarkable. From 2015 to 2016, podcast ad revenues increased 73 percent. From 2016 to 2017 revenues increased again by 85 percent to reach a total of $220 million for 2017.[28]

The growth is explosive, and many podcasts are wildly successful, reaching millions of self-selected viewers around the country. Podcast topics have enormous range, from human interest, music, and sports to pop culture, fiction, and politics. But it's that last topic—politics—that's experiencing dramatic growth.

Crooked Media is the name of a media company founded by former Obama White House staffers, one of whom was also involved in Hillary Clinton's 2008 presidential campaign. After being shocked and disappointed by the results of the 2016 election, they decided to do something about it, creating Crooked Media (inspired by Donald Trump's insulting nickname for mainstream media outlets and journalists) to spread a politically progressive message in audio form.[29] While they weren't taken seriously at first—indeed, the team didn't take themselves too seriously—on their flagship podcast *Pod Save America*, which features cover art of George Washington wearing Apple earbuds, they did have a serious message. Their audience realized that though they had a goofy twist, they were serious people. The founders and hosts of *Pod Save America* are two former speechwriters for President Obama, his former national security spokesman, and his former communications director. Enjoying an incredibly successful 2017, Crooked Media quickly expanded into a progressive answer to right-wing outrage, rolling out new podcast shows such as *Pod Save the World* on foreign policy; *Pod Save the People* on progressive social issues such as race and gender; *With Friends Like These,* featuring thoughtful discussions with people who have different political opinions; *Majority54*, which engages with Trump voters; *Keep It*, a pop culture podcase, and *Lovett or Leave It*, a political game show. The entire Crooked Media podcast suite is consistently near the top of the podcast charts and reaches millions of Americans several times a week. It's a destination for political candidates across the left, for sitting members of Congress and Senators (Cory Booker, Kristen Gillibrand, and Kamala

Harris have all appeared), and they've even interviewed Barack Obama and Hillary Clinton.[30]

What's fascinating about Crooked Media in the political and advertising landscape is how they don't shy away from controversy. They seek out productive conflict and try to engage outside their base, but they have powerfully strong opinions, and they make them known. They're known for their uncensored approach and are proud of their explicit rating, using vulgarity and profanity to castigate their political opponents. Their popularity in the country has skyrocketed, and they've toured across the country and even to Europe. Their listeners love it. So do their advertisers. The Crooked Media team has fun reading their sponsors' content, and listeners have come to associate products such as Harry's razors, Parachute sheets, and the Cash App, with a progressive agenda they deeply care about. It's not just the listeners, but also in part the sponsors, who have made the Crooked Media movement possible. It's a great example of adapting to a medium and engaging with a cause instead of co-opting it.

Social Media and Corporate Social Responsibility

In the era before social media, companies might have found themselves guessing or using focus groups to try to determine the direction in which public values might guide them. But in the era of social media, there's no reason why that should continue to be true. The values of young millennials and Generation Z are inherently knowable. They broadcast them on social media every day, generating mountains of data that companies can use to understand their customer base. Indeed, social media platforms such as Twitter are actually built with the very goal of trackable trends. It takes a matter of hours, rather than days or weeks, to judge public response to an event in the news. When it comes to corporate social responsibility, too, millennials aren't shy about using social media to engage and to express their opinions.

Two-thirds of millennials use social media to engage around corporate social responsibility (66 percent versus 53 percent of the US on average).[31]

The millennial corporate conscience extends well into their own lives, taking a more self-reflective approach than the generation before them. This conscience bleeds into the job hunt, too. Sixty-two percent of millennials are willing to take a pay cut to work for a responsible company. While this might not, on its face, inform marketing strategy, it does still provide valuable information. It tells us how much millennials, and by extrapolation the generation after them, care about corporate social responsibility.[32]

The numbers broadly bear out this understanding of the millennial consumer conscience. According to a Georgetown Center for Social Impact Communication study, "Eighty-one percent of Americans believe corporations should take action to address important issues facing society, and 88 percent believe corporations have the power to influence social change." Global numbers reflect an even stronger trend: "Eight-five percent of global consumers say how a company responds to issues and crises is an important factor in their opinion of the organization overall."[33] This particular point—responding to issues and crises—is a crucial one. In this chapter, we'll be coming back it over and over again, not just because it bears repeating, but because corporate *responses* to cultural events are a key issue facing corporate decision makers, and it can have a critical effect on perceptions. Later, we'll examine some concrete examples of corporations responding to social crises. But first, let's focus on our understanding of an activist framework and why silence is no longer an option.

Activism: Shining a Light on Corporate Blind Spots

Activism is a new paradigm of corporate investment. In unprecedented ways, it influences how investment decisions are made, streams guided, and goals targeted. Activist investors are hugely important figures. They have the assets that can change the fortunes of companies, especially smaller businesses in the post-startup phase. They also have the time, resources, and interest to analyze in great depth the way a company does business to gain a better idea of whether it's a place they want to put their money. One of the calculations such an investor will make is how responsive companies are to social pressures. If an investor fears a company might lose business because of practices that its customers wouldn't approve of, it's an easy decision to take their investment elsewhere.

Investment activism has generally evolved over two stages. In the past, investors would make their financial analyses, determined whether an investment is safe or not, then made the decision to invest or not. Once they became a major stakeholder in the company and had gained a certain degree of influence, they considered themselves to be in a position to make a statement of their interests, and perhaps thereafter have an influence on policy.

Big data analytics and the ability to watch public perception evolve in real time has fundamentally changed this way of doing business and had an impact on how investment operates. In this new phase, investors want to see businesses take careful consideration of how they're publicly perceived—how they react to crises, how they address major issues in politics and society. And these investors are not shy about how they expect companies to conduct themselves. This changing dynamic has had such an effect that investors now issue statements of values before even undertaking the decision to make an investment. They want companies to have a clear understanding of what investors expect from them—to conduct thorough review of the way they do business—so they're safe and conscientious investment opportunities before the investment even lands.

The result is that mature, well-established companies are reevaluating the way they do business. They're not only shifting their approach to reflect changing values in society, but also responding to a direct and immediate financial reason. Investment remains just as important to them as ever, and older firms need to continue to be flexible and able to adapt to the marketplace. Because one of the major concerns of activist investors isn't just a solid business plan, but a socially responsible one, the new paradigm of corporate social responsibility has far-reaching consequences. Foremost among them is the new reality of this digital era. Silence is no longer an option.

Boycotting: Risk, Success, and Failure

Earlier, I discussed engagement that takes the form of consumers, often millennials, expressing their support by enthusiastically existing in a new cultural space and having new conversations. The Crooked Media phenomenon on the political left buoyed advertisers into an edgy, but comfortable, political space where there's a broad base of passionate support. Though the content they sponsored made politically polarizing statements, it was something their audience wanted to passionately engage with. At the same time, with such a stable base of support, those advertisers don't need to be concerned about alienating people who disagree. This type of flexibility is afforded by newer, more flexible, and dynamic digital markets.

However, in well-established analog markets, the same logic doesn't always apply. If consumers or advertisers are upset by a misstep, crisis, or bad policy, the consequences can be dynamic. Let's take a look at some examples of this effect in action, starting with the boycott.

These case studies, presented in no particular order, demonstrate the effect advertisers can have on media by showing instances of advertisers withdrawing their support for certain media due to political and social backlash. The point here isn't that advertising can determine the course or nature of broadcasting—though, of course, it can. Instead, advertisers, when they pull their advertising, aren't responding to the broadcasting content. They're responding to their shareholders and customers, who are responding to the broadcasting content. The social act we're examining isn't the boycott; the boycott is the result of the social act—corporate social responsibility in action.

One of the most prominent examples of a boycott in action occurred when advertisers began to pull their content from Fox News. The organization has been in various sets of crosshairs for years due to their conservative political leanings. But like Crooked Media on the left, they have a solid and well-established base of support. A conservative worldview never merited the sort of outrage that caused advertisers to leave, except in the notable case of Glenn Beck, who espoused views on his show that went well over the line of what even conservative viewers considered to be acceptable. In this case, Beck was broadly criticized for his use of racist dog whistles and conspiracy theories. An organized advertising boycott led by Media Matters brought his show to an end in 2011.

Bill O'Reilly was Fox News's most popular television host in 2017, and had been the network's highest-rated star for sixteen years. In a single quarter in 2017, he had as many as 3.65 million viewers; he was an incredibly influential media figure with a consistently stable base of support. But when allegations began to emerge that he exhibited a pattern of sexual harassment, outrage slowly began to build.

By the time news had broken that O'Reilly had been accused by five different women of sexual harassment on his show, and that he had settled with the women was known within the organization but never publicly disclosed, many consumers—not just viewers—had had enough. This was visible in a variety of ways. Half a million Twitter followers almost immediately rallied behind the boycott, organizing with the hashtag #DropOReilly.[34] Most tellingly, a number of brands issued statements that they would pull their advertising before activist groups even had the opportunity to formally call on them to do so. This is an incredibly significant development. It demonstrates not only that companies are willing to step up and represent their values, but also that they have redefined their corporate cultures to reflect that priority. They're not just talking the talk, they're walking the walk. And it isn't small startup advertisers such as the Crooked Media sponsors either.

BMW, Mercedes, and Hyundai were among the sponsors that pulled their advertising from O'Reilly's show. Ultimately, O'Reilly lost his show.[35] Not only do advertisers affect the media conversation, advertisers themselves are responding to public demand for social responsibility, for upholding the values they consider most important.

Fox News is an example of successful boycotting. However, sexual harassment scandals represent a fairly easy situation to judge. The decision to condemn it isn't a very difficult one. It's worth bearing in mind that the decisions are not always so easy, because the issues are not always so clear cut, even when they occupy an even greater spotlight.

A case involving public outcry, social and political pressure, and corporate responsibility that's much more difficult to adjudicate comes from a region known for its conflict and controversy: Israel and Palestine. Even the wording I choose must be carefully considered because the words carry a lot of weight, and people all over the world vehemently disagree about which ones are proper. The country of Israel's relationship with its Palestinian neighbors goes back decades, to the 1940s—according to one perspective. According to another, it goes back thousands of years. These debates are not isolated to the media, social, and corporate spheres. Blood is shed daily as a direct or indirect result of this debate, which is why it's worth careful consideration and a thoughtful approach.

Most people are familiar with the basics, and I'll try to paint as neutral a picture as I can. The Jewish state of Israel and the Arab, predominantly Muslim state of Palestine both claim the same territory. Already, I've taken a risk with my phrasing, and I've made my choice based on ease of expression. While most countries in the world consider Palestine to be a state, Israel does not, and neither does the United States. In either case, my interest here isn't to make a claim one way or the other, but to make clear how contentious of an issue this really is. Israel and Palestine both believe that, historically and rightfully, the land upon which the other sits belongs historically and rightfully to them. Israel holds the strategic upper hand. AsWith As a more developed economy and greater military power, they control both Israeli territory and the borders through which Palestinians can pass. Though Palestinians do have political autonomy in their own territory, Israel controls what goes in and out and sometimes use military force to control Palestine—or to defend themselves, depending on your perspective. Israel claims this is a necessary state of affairs, not only because countries in their neighborhood such as Iran have declared a desire to destroy Israel, but also because they're threatened by terrorist organizations within Palestine.

The result is a stalemate, but there is recent activism in the form of the Boycott, Divestment, and Sanctions (BDS) movement. BDS is an international activist movement that calls for businesses and investors to stop doing business with Israel until it improves its behavior.[36] It makes the case that Israel is violating the rights of Palestinians by restricting their economy and effectively segregating their populations in violation of their human rights. Israel, for its part, makes the case that it has the right to defend itself, and is only taking action necessary for self-preservation. Critics of the BDS movement within Israel and around the world condemn it as anti-Semitic. Americans in particular say that it's a betrayal of an important US ally. In the United States, some lawmakers even call for the BDS movement to be made illegal.[37]

The issue is extremely difficult to navigate. BDS is a clear call for corporate social responsibility to support the human rights of Palestinians, but it can also be viewed as the opposite—an *abdication* of the responsibility that corporations have to support a friend and ally. I don't have the answer, but this is a story worth telling because it demonstrates the need for a careful review and evaluation of corporate priorities. Silence, in any case, isn't an answer. Companies can neither predict nor prevent eventually being called upon to give an answer. Every company needs to take careful stock of its stance so when the time comes, it can be confident in its decision, and the public can trust the company is making the right one.[38]

Corporate Environmental Responsibility

Companies need to build greater flexibility and responsiveness into their models that allows them to react to crises and incidents as they occur. However, just as valuable as the ability to respond to events quickly and thoughtfully is the ability to claim a reason for acting. A statement of purpose helps the public understand what you stand for and feel good about supporting it. One of the defining issues of our time is corporate responsibility to the environment. Not only does environmental change have universal impact felt all around the world, it's also an area that millennials and Generation Z feel very strongly about, with good reason.

The climate change generation is coming of age, the first generation of people who learned about climate change in school as fact and didn't need to be convinced of it by science, politicians, or the media. For them, climate change is taken for granted. It's an immutable truth, and it impacts every aspect of life, all around the world, permeating everything.

Not only do the vast majority of young people understand the reality of climate change as basic fact, they also know which actors bear responsibility, and they're unwilling to be generous. It's easy to understand that pollution is a necessary part of development, and it isn't a stretch to be sympathetic to developing nations who need to produce a certain amount of carbon dioxide to attain a standard of living conducive to wellbeing. But when a country as rich as the United States continues to pollute at the level it does because of the reluctance of corporations to recognize the role they play in changing the planet's climate, young people are a great deal less forgiving.

That's why there are movements on campus to divest from fossil fuel industries, and it's why biking and greener public transportation are unprecedentedly popular among the younger generation. It's also why companies are finally seeing the light and changing the way they do business, both because it's the right thing to do and because the public understands that fact.[39]

A Case Study in the Consequence of Silence: Corporate Social Responsibility in the Age of Trump

Regardless of what your opinions might be of his presidency or his policies, the era of President Trump is by any measure characterized by greater polarization. Extreme measures or stances taken by the president and his administration have and will continue to elicit strong reactions from every side—some positive, and, judging by the numbers, many negative. To understand the causes and the consequences of corporate reactions to political events, let's examine one of the most prominent and extreme examples of President Trump's young term: the ban placed on immigrants entering the United States from seven Muslim-majority countries. Notice here how I frame the wording; I did my best to find the most neutral description I could, because the framing of an issue plays an outside role on understanding it, even if it doesn't change the issue itself. [40]

Some news outlets referred to it as a travel restriction, other commentators called it a Muslim ban, and even that difference is an indication of opinion. The ban was received with public outrage across the country, even though some members of the public and the policy making community who supported it. Those voices, along with the voice of the White House itself, were drowned out by the public outcry that followed.

Protests sprang up organically in cities all around the country, where people rushed to airports to rally around family members awaiting their loved ones. Lawyers and immigration experts offered their services to immigrants free of charge, and Senators and members of Congress were often just as upset and eager to find out what was going on. As has become the norm in the social media environment, a cascade of personal statements and responses to the ban followed as elected officials and celebrities were called upon to make their feelings known. Though it wasn't quite as immediate, eventually it fell also to companies to articulate a response to the travel ban as well. Companies had a few reasons to feel compelled to speak out.

The primary reason, and the reason that guided the initial responses, was one of moral outrage. Some companies had such an immediate and strong reaction that they felt compelled to make statements, even if they hadn't been specifically called upon to do so. These reactions were also often powerful statements, and were generally viewed positively by the public.[41] Take Starbucks, for instance, whose CEO reacted by publishing an open letter to all employees within days of the executive order being announced. The language was unequivocal: "We are witness to the conscience of our country, and of the American Dream, being called into question.... I am hearing the alarm that you are sounding that the civility and human rights we have all taken for granted for so long are under attack."[42] The letter went on to pledge support for the values threatened by the executive order and outlined concrete steps that the company planned to take, including hiring ten thousand refugees from seventy-five countries over five years.

Tim Cook, the CEO of Apple, had a similarly strong response. He made a statement reiterating the values of the company, saying, "Apple would not exist without immigration, let alone thrive and innovate the way we do."[43] He even went so far as to publicly weigh taking legal action against the ban.

Netflix CEO Reed Hastings issued an even stronger statement:

"Trump's actions are hurting Netflix employees around the world, and are so un-American it pains us all. Worse, these actions will make America less safe (through hatred and loss of allies) rather than more safe. A very sad week, and more to come with the lives of over 600,000 Dreamers here in America under imminent threat. It is time to link arms together to protect American values of freedom and opportunity."[44]

Not only did Hastings, on the day following the execution of the ban, make a swift and unequivocal condemnation of the values expressed by the travel ban, he included a call to action. Unlike Pepsi and Dodge, he didn't say Netflix was the solution to divisiveness. Instead, he called upon he audience, his employees, and his customers to *take* action and engage with a cause instead of ride it or co-opt it. [45]

Lyft, the ride-sharing app, also issued a statement condemning the ban as "antithetical to both Lyft's and our nation's core values." [46] It pledged to donate $1 million to the American Civil Liberties Union. Here, we see the type of action that elicits a positive response from the media as well as from customers in the industry. From the positive attention that companies received due to their quick and firm criticism of the travel ban, we can see that there is indeed value in speaking out, even if the issue is controversial. The most important thing is to ask the high-value question: not how to avoid controversy, but how to use a powerful moment to advance your corporate values.

Purpose-Driven Companies: A New Paradigm of Corporate Mission

The concept of entropy states that no matter how much we try to organize information, order always tends towards disorder. It requires energy to organize information and matter and far less energy for chaos to take hold. Imagine trying to scrape together a pile of sand. There will always be some corner giving way, some miniature rockslide taking place. It requires concentration to keep things together. All it requires is a lapse in concentration to allow a gust of wind to blow everything apart. In this way, information is the same as sand: it wants to be released, it exists to be known. Silence isn't a natural state. A purpose-driven company understands this and works toward the goal of expression, not concealment of information because it knows that just like life in Jurassic Park: information finds a way.

Purpose-driven companies can be responsive to markets. Indeed, the market provides a useful guide for how a company can best fulfill its mission. If employee turnover is low, it means employees approve of how the company operates. Remember the statistic from earlier, about millennials being willing to take a pay cut to work for company whose purpose they agree with? In the new economic paradigm of purpose-driven markets, if brand value and sales are high, this too signifies popular approval of a corporate mission. It's possible to be idealistic and still use a rational, scientific approach to achieve that idealism.

Of course, there's a huge and important difference between being responsive to changing societal values and ethics on the one hand, and letting your corporate culture be defined by outside influence on the other. If every company responded in the same way to every crisis and had the same opinion on every issue, it would be a far less dynamic market and a far less interesting world. Our value comes from our differences, and progress results from controversy, even if tension results from those differences, too. It's neither realistic nor desirable for every company to adopt the same stance and prioritize the same things—that would undermine the very nature of productive competition that gave rise to a capitalist system in the first place. It's the responsibility of individual actors to decide what they stand for, what to tolerate, and when to draw the line. Recently, it may seem as though we're asking the same thing of all actors, but that's more likely a result of the fact that recently, many headlines and issues have been so negative that the only options were to condemn them or not speak at all. Hopefully, with time, things will even back out, and there will be more nuance in the public discourse, more room for discussion and debate.

But what's becoming clearer every day is that silence is increasingly less of an option. By framing the issue as a high-value question, we understand that today's consumers and today's society *want to engage*. They want to be proud of their investments, and they want to feel good about the products they buy. It's the job of the companies that serve them to facilitate this by making their positions clear as well. Don't state a vision; state a purpose. Express support where appropriate, condemnation where necessary, and contribute to society over everything else.

Q	How do I ensure my brand is perceived as socially responsible?
B	I believe in the value of environmental sustainability.
A	1. Divest from fossil fuels to support renewable energy. 2. Streamline my supply chain to reduce waste. 3. Launch a top-to-bottom recycling initiative.
M	1. Measure with focus groups whether my environmentally sustainable message reaches consumers. 2. Measure with surveys whether the decision to purchase detracts from my environmental initiatives.

Table 4: QBAM for Corporate Responsibility

CHAPTER THIRTEEN

Is Securing My Data Trustworthy Enough?

THE IOT IS BECOMING more pervasive, and consequently, more significant. Big data is taking an increasingly prominent role, and because of that, the IoT is shifting to the Internet of Trust. It's happening already.

Move Beyond Security and Data Integrity: The Internet of Trust

By 2020, between 20 and 30 billion devices will be connected to the IoT. The current count is between 6.4 billion and 17.6 billion, depending on whether you include computers, tablets, and smartphones.[47]

Regardless, the numbers are staggering because of what they indicate and the potential they represent, especially related to how they'll influence business strategy. The billions of devices—some of which aren't yet invented or publicly available—will generate data and analytics that will ultimately drive automated and policy-based decisions. These business decisions will become immensely important as they affect safety, production and productivity levels, and billions of dollars.

Data safety is important. But is your data safe enough to drive explosive adoption of the IoT and realize the value foretold by me and by other experts? When you apply the principles of Questioneering, I believe there's a high-value question. Most companies ask the low-value question: "Is the data secure?" But think about what this question assumes. Because it asks about safety, it assumes the data is valuable. But what makes data valuable? The assumption that it's correct? *Aha!* This extrapolation leads us to the high-value question that we should be asking instead. The high-value question of the near future will be: *Is my data trustworthy?* The conversation will shift from *Is the data secure?* to *Is the data correct? Is it* actually *right?* This is what's behind the Internet of Trust.

Consider the implications if the data you use is actually wrong. Maybe it's been manipulated purposely. Or maybe there's some other kind of contextual event—maybe the global temperature rises or something takes place in the environment—but the data has changed. Data that's wrong can have disastrous effects for both the business and the consumer. At the very least, it erodes trust, causing customers to leave. But it can have larger implications, some of which we'll examine more closely later this chapter.

The kind of thing I'm talking about starts with basic quality checks and goes much further. But for now, consider the CNN graphic for the vote on Scotland's referendum for independence a few years ago. The graphic reported 58 percent of voters had voted yes, while 52 percent had voted no. See the problem? Add up the percentages and you get 110 percent of voters. To make matters worse, the majority of voters had actually voted no![48] Of course, CNN corrected itself, but the error had already been captured and filled the social media airwaves in no time. When credibility takes just a second to destroy, it's worth taking the time to ensure that data is correct.

The reality is this: for people to trust the IoT and truly automate, for them to take action on what connected devices tell them to do, they need to trust the data. The Internet of Trust will take center stage. Here's where blockchain technology, which inherently resists data corruption, comes in. A compelling case can be made for data integrity in the financial services industry, which has plenty of opportunities for fraud and crime. Blockchain technology is being put to use in global supply chains to increase traceability, reducing imports of counterfeit and pirated goods. This technology will help guide the Internet of Trust.

How Data Quality Influences Consumer Trust and Use

It's almost stating the obvious to say consumers expect security, and businesses should have strategies in place to provide it. Security has become table stakes. What's increasingly evident is that real value for organizations emerges from the opportunities accurate data presents.

Consumers are the driving force behind this realization, as the trust they have in data steers the degree to which they decide to interact with it. We know people are more aware than ever of the kinds of personal details that they can choose to provide on websites and apps. They have come to understand that there's value in those details.

By extension, consumers are much more likely to pay attention to how businesses use their personal information and when any misuse takes place. Because consumers are alert to how they may benefit from any data they share, the consequences of having inaccurate data have also become more dramatic.

None of this is news to organizations. Nearly three-quarters of businesses are aware that data quality issues affect customer trust and perception. And the losses are real, in terms of both revenue and reputation. One estimate suggests that, in 2015, organizations lost more than $8.8 million annually due to data quality issues. We know the stakes around data have only escalated since then. Organizations need to learn how to stem the losses and take their relationships with consumers to a more stable, productive level. [49]

All it takes is a high-profile hack to remind consumers to pay attention to how their information is being used. They'll immediately question what kinds of protection are in place, even as they may be surprised to learn the depth of personal details kept on file.

Consider the high-profile Equifax data breach, which exposed the personal information of 145.5 million customers in September 2017. Months later, it came to light that personal details such as tax identification numbers, phone numbers, and email addresses had been exposed, along with names, birthdates, Social Security numbers and, to some extent, credit card numbers and driver's license numbers.[50]

The issue here isn't just the additional exposure for consumers. It's that more information has come to light, which can further erode the already-compromised trust consumers have in Equifax. The company didn't disclose the hack for months after it took place, and its handling of the lapse fell short, with customer service representatives who couldn't answer anxious consumers' questions, a website that demonstrated questionable security protocols, and a generally ineffective communications strategy.

Is it too late for customers to grant the goodwill that they often do in the case of a security breach or lapse of trust? We know 51 percent of consumers will forgive a consumer product company that had a single data breach of their personal data as long as the company addressed the issue quickly.[51]

The bottom line in today's marketplace is that consumers expect their data to be protected if companies collect and use it. By extension, they also expect it to be used in a way that benefits them, whether that means greater convenience, exclusive content, targeted offers, loyalty rewards, or some other premier treatment, including privacy protection. If their expectations are met, they'll verify, update, add to, and otherwise interact with their information. That kind of interaction is the value they give back to the organization. That's the organization's reward.

Think about music services such as Pandora that create playlists based on a user's listening history. The playlists are created based on how a user behaves, including how many times they listen to a track, how many similar tracks they listen to, what they search for, and on and on. This type of personalization isn't new. Remember the first time Amazon's "Recommended for You" feature popped up on your browser?

Each time a person likes something on Facebook or indicates interest in an article they read on LinkedIn, they share data. The more accurately Facebook and LinkedIn mine that data to make recommends for newsfeeds, connections, and groups, the more engaged and loyal that person is likely to be. Let me say it again: this kind of data is integral to shaping the business strategy of the near future. An Experian report found 70 percent of organizations believe that by 2020, customer data will drive the majority of sales decisions.[52]

A 2017 Global Consumer Trust report identifies consumer behaviors that can tip off organizations about consumer trust and decision making. The report surveyed 6,500 smartphone users in ten global markets about why they do and don't use certain apps and programs.

Their responses reveal core consumer issues around trust organizations can use to shape strategy:

1. Forty percent named one or more trust issues as the most important barrier to not using more apps and services.
2. The most influential trust-related concern is privacy (16 percent), followed by security (15 percent).
3. Transparency is key: Thirty-three percent say a clear, simple privacy statement makes an app or service trustworthy.
4. Organizations most trusted to manage data are banks and credit cards (46 percent) and doctors and hospitals (45 percent). At the same time, consumers consider financial details the most sensitive.
5. Fifty-three percent of smartphone users in the survey know they're not in control of how their data is used.
6. Consumers said privacy protection and access to their data outweigh financial and other rewards as exchanges for providing personal data.[53]

What do these responses tell us about the drivers behind and the impact of trust? Transparency is important, because it reassures consumers about what's being done—and not done—with the information they provide. Even though consumers understand their data is being funneled along with that of all other consumers, they want it to remain private. When they provide their birthdate, age, or preferences, they assume they're entering a trust contract with the organization. And again, they expect something in return.

Here's the bottom line: consumers want assurance that their information stays confidential and accessible. If they have that, they'll participate more vigorously in providing data because they'll be enjoying a good user experience. That's the absolute foundation of every data strategy within the Internet of Trust.

Surprise! A Gap Exists Between Consumer and Business Executive Beliefs

If organizations want to collect accurate data—if they want to participate in the Internet of Trust—they must give consumers what they need, which is assurance that the risks of sharing personal information are worth it. However, huge gaps exist between what consumers believe to be true and what executives believe to be true in this area.

A 2014 Deloitte study indicates 25 percent of consumers believe the risks of sharing personal information is worth the personalized advertising, coupons, or promotions they receive. Eighteen percent of consumers believe sharing is worth the product recommendations they receive. Put otherwise, 75 to 82 percent of consumers believe personalized offers or recommendations do *not* outweigh the perceived risks of sharing information.

Those are significant numbers in and of themselves. But what makes them really interesting and worth taking notice, is that 47 percent of executives believe the risks of sharing personal information *are* worth the personalized offers or recommendations.[54]

There's a monumental gap between what executives believe about consumers and what consumers themselves believe. It's huge. Organizations are overestimating consumer comfort with sharing personal data, along with the degree to which consumers feel the benefits they receive are worth it. Organizations are out of touch, and the gap between what consumers believe and what organizations perhaps wish they would believe is significant. As we discussed in the first two sections of this book, challenge what you believe to be true.

To have an edge, organizations must listen to consumers and create purposeful data strategies that result in accurate data. I may sound like a broken record here, but accurate data means trust, and trust means more insights into consumers' lives and preferences, which gives an organization a competitive advantage.

PwC reports 64 percent of CEOs surveyed globally cite data management as a key differentiating factor in the future.[55] Forward-thinking companies see the big picture and have started to integrate services with data by beefing up their menu of offerings and products. They're gaining critical competitive advantage while offering customers new value.

Think about Alphabet, Google's parent company, and how it can integrate all the data from the two hundred companies it owns, including its search engine, its Chrome browser, Google Maps, and YouTube. Information is power, and organizations that build trust upon personal data will have the edge.

How Bad Data Affects Organizations

Bad data is real. More than 70 percent of companies report data quality concerns affect customer trust and perception, with more than 60 percent indicating that inaccurate data currently undermines their ability to provide an excellent customer experience. And more than 80 percent of companies are struggling to create a single customer view (SCV), which consolidates all the data about a customer into a single record, whether they're using a smartphone, computer, or tablet, regardless of when and where they're using their device.[56]

Organizations are running behind consumers in their relationships with data, and they have their marching orders. They must absolutely, positively create sound data management strategies to collect the information they need to gather and retain customers. They also need accurate data to navigate the enormous volume of data within the IoT—more on that later.

Here's a mind-numbing figure: IBM estimates poor data quality costs the US economy approximately $3.1 *trillion* annually.[57] Trillion—you read that right, and that's *just* the United States! As a point of comparison, consider that International Data Corporation says worldwide revenues for big data and business analytics will grow from $130.1 billion in 2016 to more than $203 billion in 2020.[58] The losses far outweigh the revenues, which means opportunities linked to data improvement are stunning.

Now add this to the equation: IBM also found that one in three business leaders does not trust the information they use to make business decisions.[59] What is happening? Why are one-third of business leaders making risky decisions with which they're uncomfortable? Additionally, why are they subjecting customers to poor experiences based on poor data, which undermines their whole enterprise?

Here's the short answer: improving data quality is difficult, arduous, time-consuming work, and many organizations are not structured to accommodate it properly. Writing in the *Harvard Business Review*, Thomas C. Redman notes bad data is expensive because so many people must accommodate it day to day. This includes people at every level in an organization, from decision makers to knowledge workers to data scientists.

Working with inferior data costs time and money. And because every person in an organization is working under pressure, Redman notes, many people just make corrections themselves to complete the task at hand. They don't have time or perhaps don't think to touch base with the person who created the data, explain what they need, and help fix the underlying problem.[60]

Originators of the data are typically far removed from the consequences of bad data. In a relatively simple case, this means a package gets delivered to the wrong address. In a more complex case that could have disastrous consequences, someone gets the wrong medicine in a prescription.

Few organizations are immune to data accuracy woes. An Irish study of seventy-five executives found data quality is in worse shape than they realized. Just 3 percent of those executives found their departments fell within a minimum acceptable range of ninety-seven or more correct records out of one hundred. Furthermore, on average, 47 percent—nearly half—of new data records have at least one critical error that impacts work.[61]

Doing the hard work of anticipating and fixing data issues will help you avoid events that can lose your customers' trust in a millisecond. One example is the infamous mailing OfficeMax sent to a customer, addressed to "Mike Seay, Daughter Killed in Car Crash." Indeed, Seay's daughter had died in a car crash one year earlier. The fact that OfficeMax had the data is one thing—they collected data they didn't really need. But that the organization didn't weed it out is a potential deal breaker for countless customers when the error went viral.[62]

Let's consider what actually constitutes good data, understanding that every organization has its own needs, nuances, and goals. As a decision maker, you must become familiar with data so you can determine whether it meets your expectations. You need to trust that data as though it's your lifeline, because it is.

If you've been listening to and reading the landscape around you, you'll know relatively quickly whether data matches up with the things you know to be true. If it doesn't match, you might have a data problem—or an opportunity. It depends on how you've collected and utilized your data.

A Forbes Insights report notes good data can be assessed for accuracy, completeness, standardization, and authority.[63] Accuracy means that the data is correct, whether a mailing label gets a package to its proper destination or whether data points are timely. The degree of accuracy depends on how closely it matches its intended use.

If you have multiple addresses for a customer, they might all be right. But if your system sends a package to the customer's home, where you send Christmas cookies as a thank you gift, when it should have gone to the warehouse, you have an accuracy issue. Or, if your mailing list has duplicates and a customer receives multiple annual reports, they'll perceive you as indulgent and perhaps sloppy; at the same time, you're spending money you don't have to on those extra mailings.

Complete data is indicated by its inverse, which is incomplete data. What if you're trying to track how many times a person stays at your luxury hotel line in a year? If your software registers only a portion of those stays, you'll miss out on determining who your A-list customers are, and you're failing to provide a good customer experience.

You need standardized data to set up comparisons. Telephone numbers in the United States are formatted in a different way than telephone numbers in England, as are street addresses. You need the ability to standardize input and transform data so you can compare customers accurately.

Authoritative data means your data draws from a credible and appropriate source. The US Census Bureau is an example of an authoritative external source for demographic information. Ensuring your source is reliable helps ensure output that's trustworthy.

The same Forbes Insights report offers more details about how good and bad data affect an organization.[64] Remember, we already know how data can help provide a good customer experience, lead to new products and services and increase efficiency. Consider these benefits:

1. **Better decisions**: Good-quality data ensures less risk and guesswork, which means more efficiency and more confidence. There's no way to argue with outcomes based on good data.

2. **Increased productivity**: If data is clean, no one in the organization has to spend time fixing it or cleaning up after it. They can do their jobs and move forward.

3. **Compliance**: In some industries, accurate data can save an organization hefty fines that can run into the millions of dollars. Compliance laws also shift, so data must be structured to respond appropriately.

4. **Marketing**: Organizations can track their customers as they shop on their phones, in the retail store, and on their computers at home. The data collected within such an omnichannel sales approach builds the advanced analytics that provide critical insights for marketing strategies. Today's organizations can personalize marketing to an amazing degree, delivering unbelievable customer experiences. But those experiences won't be memorable in the right ways unless the data is absolutely right.

For as liberating as good data can be, bad data can be equally, if not more damaging:

1. **Undermined confidence**: A global survey by KPMG found 84 percent of CEOs have concerns about the quality of data on which they base decisions.[65] If you can't make decisions based on data, what will you use to make decisions? Forbes Insights quotes Attain Insights CEO Paul Hulford on the problem with defaulting to tried-and-true methods: "Like anything else, when people don't trust the system, they look to other ways of making decisions. They may move back to traditional techniques—opinions from trusted individuals, instinct, experience—and while those things are very important, they're also open to interpretation and vulnerability.... So the cost for companies

that put less emphasis on analytics and more emphasis on instinct is that they'll be putting the organization at greater risk."[66] As we have discussed previously, data is a critical component of building your formalized approach to listening.

2. **Missed opportunities**: The more you understand how to use data to your advantage, the further ahead of your competition you are. Your data can lead you to your next brilliant service. Don't miss out on it and let someone else have it.

3. **Lost revenue**: Faulty data can affect revenue in countless ways. Mailings are one of the preeminent ways. Let's say one-third of your mailing list is bad; you have lost one-third of your revenue potential. United Airlines uses a legacy software system that's so out of date, the airline loses nearly $1 billion a year in revenue—a significant amount, even with approximately $37 billion in sales. The software is so outdated, it doesn't provide accurate assumptions about how much travelers will pay for a seat or forecast demand well for small markets. The airline is fixing the problem and expects smarter pricing in the future will generate an additional $900 million in revenue by 2020.[67]

4. **Damaged reputation**: Not every organization knows when its reputation has taken a hit with an individual customer. But social media rankings are a good barometer and are surprisingly accurate. In other cases, reputations can take a very public, notable dive based on inaccurate data. Amazon's reputation in the electronics market took a hit after it introduced the ill-fated Fire Phone in 2014. There were misfires with pricing, features, operating system software, and carrier contracts. Amazon reduced the price of the phone from $200 to $0.99 one month after its unveiling.[68] It's fair to assume Amazon will review data more carefully, or at least differently, in its next venture into phones.

As the stakes related to data increase for organizations, the need to get data right is underscored by new and emerging regulations. The European Union's General Data Protection Regulation (GDPR) expands consumer rights and gives organizations more responsibility. In the case of a data breach, an organization must notify its customers within seventy-two hours. If companies don't comply with the GDPR, regulators in Europe may fine them up to €20 million ($24.6 million) or 4 percent of total worldwide annual revenue of the preceding financial year, whichever is higher.[69]

While some details are still not entirely clear, what's evident is that consumer consent is vital to compliance. Once again, we return to an understanding that consumers want transparency about how their information will be used and some control over it, too.

Compliance and regulation are driving forces in data management, but they're not the sum of their parts. Certainly, businesses need to develop mature data management strategies. But they also need to recognize that by complying with regulations, and by extension providing customers with more value, they can develop value for themselves.

Experian notes that 69 percent of businesses who have invested in data quality solutions say they have seen a positive return on investment.[70] Maybe their sales increased, or maybe their leaders feel more confident in the decisions they've made. Perhaps their mailings are more effective, or they're working on a product that will revolutionize the world after they've clean up their data.

In any case, quality data solutions, as we have seen, put the customers' needs and desires first. They may be formulated in response to a regulation, or as a reaction to a public failure or a private insight. One thing they all share is a tie to trust. Key to the Internet of Trust is the technology that can help assure customers about data integrity: blockchain.

How the IoT Instills Trust Through Blockchain Technology

The financial services industry is a key area for data integrity because its transactional flow presents plenty of opportunities for fraud and crime. It's no surprise, then, that financial services is one of the earliest industries to adopt blockchain technology. The technology is also being used in various global supply chains, whether in the food industry or retail, because it helps ensure details such as date stamps and inspections are correct and cannot be altered.

Blockchain is a digital ledger. It implements algorithms that validate and authenticate transactions in a decentralized architecture protected by digital encryption. Each transaction resists tampering and is auditable, time-stamped, and permanent. Each new transaction on the ledger is recorded in real time and the entire ledger is updated. Blockchain technology can digitize any kind of asset. It's the birthplace of cryptocurrency, which is a marker of the technology's potential. In 2017, venture capital investors put more than $1 billion into the cryptocurrency market.[71]

With its components of transparency and accountability, blockchain provides control over digital identities that other technologies cannot. And if we're talking about trust, let's remember how consumers yearn to have control over their personal information. Blockchain provides unprecedented digital assurance in areas that include asset protection, payment processing, supply chain management, and personal information.

In the trust economy, transactions are overwhelmingly digital. Think about your daily life. You don't want to wait weeks for paperwork to come through on a new home purchase. You want to know that the fresh fish at your favorite restaurant was indeed caught yesterday. You want to transfer money to a family member instantly via a payment app. You want each and every one of these points of digital information transfer to be correct.

On a broader scale, if you're using an autonomous vehicle, you want to trust that it's safe, and the data it's using is correct. If you're a musician, you want to know that you receive the proper royalties when your songs are played. If you're an insurance agent, you want to avoid paying duplicate claims on the same accident. The structure of blockchain assures data veracity in each of these cases and in many others.

Defense giant Lockheed Martin has started to integrate blockchain technology into its supply chain risk management with GuardTime. With the effort, Lockheed Martin has become the first US defense contractor to incorporate blockchain into its developmental processes.[72]

Many drivers already question the GPS in their cars. They use it, but at times, they also doubt the directions it gives them. As autonomous vehicles become prevalent, the stakes rise. You want to be sure that when you're at a crosswalk, the car will see kids walking in that crosswalk. As the stakes grow much higher, companies will begin to differentiate around trust. How fast is the car able to make decisions? How does it know? There will be a lot more emphasis around trust as a differentiator.

Security is clearly important, but as I've noted, it'll be much more focused around trust, through technology, agreements, and marketing. For example, will your insurance rates be the same if you use an autonomous vehicle, or will they go down (or up!)? The more clearly companies can answer this question based on blockchain data, the more trust they'll earn from consumers.

Returning to the financial industry, blockchain can ensure that payments, including international transfers, are secure. Blockchain technology reduces accounting and auditing errors because blockchain is extremely secure by nature. Banks can verify customer identities more quickly because records are stored once. Blockchain reduces fraud because records can't be altered once they're recorded. In every one of these cases, both efficiency and safety skyrocket. Both are key components in a good customer experience based on trust.

Estimates suggest that by 2027, and perhaps sooner, 10 percent of the world's gross domestic product (GDP) will be stored on blockchain technology.[73] With 2027 just a few years away, think about how disruptive that shift will be. According to the World Economic Forum, financial services will include more emerging markets. New services will come to into existence, created only on the blockchain. Because the blockchain hosts all kinds of value exchanges, the number of tradable assets will magnify exponentially. The system is more inclusive, transparent, and rife with possibilities. Think about paying your income taxes on the blockchain—it may be a possibility in the future.

Another industry where data accuracy is integral is the healthcare industry, which has also started shifting toward blockchain technology. Approximately 16 percent of healthcare executives expected to implement a commercial blockchain solution in 2017.[74] Again, the potential disruption is enormous, industry-wide.

An IBM report notes that accurate records mean more accurate diagnoses and fewer errors, whether in recording notes or issuing a prescription. Treatments can be more medically effective and more cost-effective. Public health data can be shared worldwide, accurately. Drugs can be tracked from supplier to patient, accurately.[75]

What a relief all of this will be to healthcare professionals and to consumers. An accurate system means people won't have to experience the potential nightmare of erroneous medical records. We've all heard stories. Some of them can be fairly innocuous, such as the woman whose doctor asked about her two children during their first appointment. The problem with that friendly question is that the woman has no children. The doctor's information was incorrect. Do you think the patient returned to that doctor and healthcare system?

Other medical records mix-up stories are nightmares, such as a patient who wasn't supposed to eat solid food but got served a tray of it, or a patient who was short of breath but received another patient's cardiac clearance. In both cases, outcomes were poor and caused a monumental erosion of trust.[76]

It's absolutely clear that the opportunity to assure consumers about the accuracy of their data will only get stronger. The blockchain market size is expected to grow from $210.2 million in 2016 to $231.25 *billion* by 2021.[77]

Another component around trust is edge computing, which helps ensure data processing takes place in fractions of seconds and that communication interaction is correct. The voracious appetite for data that the IoT produces has pushed more network and data management strategies to the edge. The edge computing market is expected to reach $33.75 billion by 2023 at a compound annual growth rate of 35 percent.[78] In this case, speed will ensure trust by kicking out faster, more reliable data analysis.

Is there any doubt that the concerns about data and trust are worthy of some time and consideration? I don't think so. Making the right decision about technology can ensure the right adoption strategies and ultimately, success. Now that we have convinced you of the high-value question of building trust, what should you do?

Manage Data to Ensure Competitive Advantage

Whatever your industry, your consumers need assurances about data reliability, period. A Gartner study predicts three significant security and trust scenarios for the near future:

1. By 2022, most people in mature economies will consume more false information than true information. Gartner warns that while artificial intelligence (AI) is proving to be very effective in creating new information, it's just as effective at distorting data to create false information. This could result in a major financial fraud, for example, with no internet company providing an adequate solution.

2. By the end of 2020, the banking industry will derive $1 billion or more in business value from blockchain-based cryptocurrencies. In

2017, Gartner estimated the current combined value of cryptocurrencies in circulation worldwide is $155 billion. This value has been increasing as tokens continue to proliferate and market interest grows. The study suggests cryptocurrencies will represent more than half of worldwide blockchain global business value-add through 2023.

3. By 2020, AI-driven creation of counterfeit reality, or fake content, will outpace AI's ability to detect it, fomenting digital distrust. Already, AI and machine learning systems can categorize image content faster and more accurately than humans can. Imagine a counterfeit video that launches public debate after being accepted as real by one or both sides of the political spectrum. The report suggests commercial efforts to detect fake news will increase ten-fold by 2020.[79]

Each of these scenarios seems plausible, given the opportunity-driven environment regarding issues of trust. Whether the scenarios with be realized or not, they should prompt significant conversations as organizations form data management strategies.

There's not really time to wait. In 2017, 58 percent of respondents to PwC's CEO survey said they worry that a lack of trust in the business would harm their company's growth prospects, up from 37 percent in 2013.[80] There's truly no time like the present to get your organization's data in shape so you can move forward with a competitive advantage, with trust as a foundational driver.

You'll save yourself stories such as the one a large financial institution experienced. Their customer service representatives cavalierly entered salutations such as, "What an idiot John Doe is" into a database salutation field. You guessed it: when the marketing department sent out a mailing, it included letters that said, "Dear Idiot John Doe." Disastrous? Absolutely.[81]

A Deloitte report[82] offers some key ways that can help you position your organization to excel in data management:

1. **Vision and strategy**: If data management isn't an organization-wide priority, it won't be accurate. You must have buy-in at all levels and resource support. Map out a strategy to collect and use the data, and be ready to address a breach. Prepare to compensate consumers for security lapses and plan to regain their trust. Show your consumers you care about them and see them as more than mere sources of data. The Deloitte report gives an excellent example of how preparation can make a difference. In 2000, American Express (AMEX) was hacked, exposing the information of 15,000 customers. Ironically, the hack took place the day after AMEX announced their new tools to safeguard online shoppers' privacy. But AMEX had a plan and collaborated with other industry organizations to take action that included establishing a worldwide network for fraud prevention. Instead of crashing after a hack, AMEX emerged as a privacy leader thanks to their plan and preparedness.

2. **Policies**: Be sure the policies customers see are clear and easy to understand, recalling once more that transparency is vital in consumers' perceptions of trust. Consumers should be able to easily understand how to opt in and opt out of their data being used. Shift your mindset to think about your privacy policies as a marketing tool and present them accordingly in your materials, including your website. Train everyone in your organization to understand how data should be used and retained. Monitor policies so they stay up to date. Data management is a dynamic strategy, not a one-time effort.

3. **Organization and people**: Do you have a chief or senior privacy officer who has real authority to act and deliver cultural change? If you want to send a message to your organization and consumers that trust matters to you, you should. It's a tangible signal that you're ready to lead on data privacy concerns.

4. **Processes and systems**: When something goes wrong with data

and customers find out, they don't care why it happened or who is ultimately responsible. Minimize the risk of any data breach or other disaster by understanding where your risks are and putting supporting processes in place across your entire enterprise. Restrict data access on a need-to-know basis and track it. Test your systems and keep them updated.

5. **Risk management**: Know what attackers are up to and shore up your systems appropriately. Develop a risk management plan that addresses both internal and external threats, which includes third-party providers. Believe your data is vulnerable, find the flaws, and fix them.

Let's face it: organizations like to protect themselves and are filled with people who are humans, and humans often take the easiest, tried path. Rather than liberating, change is seen as threatening. We've all been there. But to survive in the world of the Internet of Trust, it's imperative that organizations prove to consumers that they can deliver correct data. Activate a sensible strategy starting now.

Let's return to the high-value question, *Is my data trustworthy?* Answering "yes" gives your organization a competitive edge. It really is that simple.

Let's look at how this plays within the QBAM framework.

Q	Is my data trustworthy?		
B	Consequences of inaccurate data drive loss of revenue and reputation.		
	Customers trust accurate data.	Data accuracy positively affects organization.	Data management strategies provide cleaner data.
A	1. Assess customer trust. 2. Provide transparency. 3. Encourage customer digital interaction.	1. Design blockchain strategy. 2. Establish security as differentiator. 3. Assure data veracity.	1. Implement organization-wide plan. 2. Continually monitor and update plan. 3. Ensure transparent processes.
M	1. Customers provide more personal information. 2. Customer interaction increases.	1. Better decisions. 2. Increased productivity. 3. Meet compliance standards.	1. Improved customer retention. 2. Increased sales.

Table 5: QBAM for Data Trustworthiness

Once again, understand what you're trying to achieve. Align the answers to the beliefs to be turned into facts. You'll build momentum that drives you right to breakthrough innovation and becoming a trust leader.

We Fear the Unknown

We often fear what we don't understand. One of the great universal intergenerational traditions is the anxiety that comes along with generational transitions. The aging generation is never comfortable with the quirks and characteristics of their children: their pastimes, entertainment, values, and ethics. These fears are plainly visible in everyday public conversations about generational values, in books and op-eds, on the news, and around the kitchen table.

Let's compare the generational trends in the twentieth century with those developing in the twenty-first. Americans who lived through the Great Depression were afraid their children wouldn't know the value of a dollar and take everything they had for granted. This would inevitably result, they feared, in a weaker society, characterized by complacency, without the grit that brought America out the other side of the worst financial crisis the country, indeed, the world, had yet experienced. But as every child learns in school, the opposite proved true in the following decade, when American ingenuity and production catapulted the economy back into the black, and the country into superpower status emerging from World War II.

But the skepticism over generational transitions continued. The battle-tested heroes who returned triumphantly from Europe, having saved the continent from the specter of fascism, didn't think their children would exhibit the same fortitude to maintain the nation's hard-earned status. They saw the younger generation enthralled by the immodesty of new trends, what we now consider to be cultural touchstones such as Elvis, Little Richard, and Chuck Berry. But instead of a distracted workforce, the era gave rise to the most famous generation yet: the baby boomers, who revived the global economy, united the Western world, and defeated the Soviet Union.

In cases like these, not only did the newest generations and the issues their parents feared turn out not to be so bad, their overwhelmingly positive impact is still recognized, felt, and studied today. Take rock 'n' roll. In the 1950s, parents thought the vulgarity and sexual overtones of popular music would cause immorality in their kids. They feared the possibility of their children dressing like greasers, going cruising, and dancing promiscuously, all evil possibilities that could result from this new, unsettling kind of music. Now think about how absurd that seems in retrospect. Rock n' roll singers from the time are icons of an era that we worship as playing a role in defining our culture. Elvis's home is now a museum. People make pilgrimages to his grave.

But there's an even more important story here. Rock n' roll went beyond simply defying the beliefs of its detractors. It became a powerful agent of change, a force for good in the world. Rock n' roll stars aren't just known today for their guitar riffs or their lyrics; their legacies transcend their talents. From this once-doubted genre emerged a movement dedicated to peace and freedom. Think of the protest songs during the Civil Rights Movement. Bob Dylan's "The Times They Are A-Changin'," "Hurricane," and "Blowin' in the Wind" imagined a freer and more just society. He used his music to help achieve it.

Billy Joel and Barry McGuire railed against the Vietnam War with "Goodnight Saigon" and "Eve of Destruction," respectively, giving a voice to a growing movement that opposed shipping young Americans off to die in an unjust war. Bruce Springsteen made history when he sang "Chimes of Freedom" in Berlin, giving those trapped in East Germany hope for a better future. David Bowie did the same, singing "Heroes" next to the Berlin Wall, listening to the voices on the other side singing joyfully and hopefully along with him.

There are dozens, if not hundreds, more examples of rock 'n' roll not just proving its detractors wrong, but having a positive effect on society. Music was once something parents feared their children listening to and encouraged them to avoid, but it became an incredibly powerful force for good and continues to be to this day.

Often, what's feared is simply misunderstood; it's both our challenge and our responsibility to try to understand. Often during a presentation, I'm approached with a question or recommendation that Questioneering isn't only for driving business innovation, but is a guide for unlocking personal success. In the next chapter, I'll share insights from leveraging the principles of Questioneering to achieve new levels of personal achievement.

CHAPTER FOURTEEN

Job Promotion or a New Level of Fulfillment?

WE OFTEN JUDGE CAREER success as the major marker of achievement. But generations have made steady changes in how they determine success to include new metrics beyond career achievements. Areas such as family, personal happiness, job security and satisfaction, and financial responsibility work in tandem with career accomplishments to establish personal success. This shift marks a change from people asking low-value questions to asking high-value questions that will bring about a greater sense of fulfillment. Instead of asking, "How do I get promoted?" people now ask, "How do I give and receive enjoyment every day of my life?"

Remember, asking high-value questions leads to high-value answers. When asking how to get promoted, you'll only derive the answer to obtain the position. But that problem comes with several Blind Spots. It assumes the path to personal or career success is through promotion. Don't get me wrong, promotion may be a step toward your goal, but it does not provide a high-value answer because there's no breakthrough moment where you learn what areas are your Blind Spots and how to challenge yourself to do more.

To really get to the nitty-gritty and define the questions you should be asking to lead to personal success, it's important to understand how success is defined. We don't all view success in the same manner, and your ideas on success are likely shaped by the values of your generation.

By understanding Questioneering as it relates to your personal success, you can adapt high-value questions that will lead to dynamic solutions for your advancement and fulfillment. Let's discuss high-value questions when interviewing, your digital persona, and the key characteristics that are shaping the future workforce.

How Do I Define Success?

Career mentor and best-selling author Bud Bilanich says, "Your definition of career success is what's right for you—not anyone else." Success is the accomplishment of your goals. Whether the goal is to attain wealth, a position in a company, an honor, or an abstract concept such as happiness, achieving a goal you set for yourself is success. It's often said that every target reached is success—small successes add up to big successes. There are many excellent novels, blogs, and articles on setting and attaining goals, but all goal setting has one thing in common: clarity of purpose.

Bilanich talks about clarity of purpose on his blog *Why You Must Define Your Own Career Success*.[83] He shares the stories of different individuals and how their clarity of purpose defined the goals that led to their personal idea of success. Knowing where you're going is essential to identifying how success is defined for you personally. When outlining what success means for you, you must know the direction in which you're heading and what marker acts as the finish line that signals attainment of the goal.

High-value questions help you figure out your end game and the steps it will take to get there. The starting line is that voice in your head that suggests you're not receiving as much fulfillment as you expected when you accomplish a goal. Sarah Denning on *Forbes* explains, "It's in those moments that the qualitative (and the most important) indicators of job satisfaction start to show,"[84] When your inner voice is speaking to you, it's time to listen.

Oftentimes, you can get high-value questions with high-value answers from your inner voice that define what success means to you. In other words, your inner voice may just hold the key to your next *aha!* moment.

What Are the Questions That Matter?

We know the definition of success is a personal decision. It's up to each person to determine goals, metrics, and success factors individually. Knowing by what metrics you gauge success will reenergize you to set achievable goals. Finding clarity of purpose is the first step to defining success, but once you have that idea, that target, it's time to start asking the high-value questions that can lead you on the path forward. It's time to start asking the questions that matter. In my discussion over the recent years, a few high-value questions have really caught my attention and led to a few personal *aha*! moments:

1. How is success defined in the digital age?
2. What is my place in the workforce of the future?
3. What questions should I be asking during interviews?
4. How can I better manage my digital persona to increase my client base?
5. What insights can I gain by how I manage my personal life and assets as compared to how top companies manage their people and important assets?

The definition of success is as personal as an opinion, and it's always changing. What Generation X thinks of as achieving success is wildly different from what millennials think. So, we must begin there. Now that we're in the digital age, how is success defined? How has it changed from one generation to the next? And what are the overarching themes? The shift from monetary success to personal fulfillment is palpable when looking through the annals of five decades worth of history on success.

As we'll find and have touched on, success is no longer just career success.

It's now about both career and personal fulfillment. To achieve a balance between career and personal fulfillment, we must ask the right questions in interviews to determine if that position aligns with our success goals, we need to address the future of the workforce—innovation, flexibility, drivers, and individualism—and we need to manage and enhance our digital personas, our public showing of what we offer. We must also look at how top companies manage their finances, relationships, and culture to advance their brand, so we can gain valuable insight into how we should manage ourselves for success.

How Do We Define Success in the Digital Age?

Technology affects everything around us, and it influences how individuals define success. From the generation that had to learn it and adapt to it, to the generation born with mobile devices in their hands, technology has shaped our values, goals, and measurements for fulfillment. Though each generation likes to think they're different from the other, there are overarching themes of success that pop up in the ideals of each generation.

No matter your generation, there are valuable insights to gain from answer the high-value question: *How is success defined by different groups of people in the digital age?* Though you may be from a certain generation, you probably work with people from the others and can better understand how they function, what meaning they find in their work, and how you can partner with them to achieve your own goals.

Generation X

Overshadowed by the baby boomers, whose massive voice called them slackers, lazy, and cynical, Generation X, born between 1961 and 1981, became synonymous with the word "lost."

Douglas Coupland offered a description of the generation on the back cover of his book *Generation X*:

"Fiercely suspicious of being lumped together as an advertiser's target market, they have quit dreary careers and cut themselves adrift.... Unsure of their futures, they immerse themselves in a regime of heavy drinking and working at McJobs.... Underemployed, overeducated, intensely private, and unpredictable, they have nowhere to direct their anger, no one to assuage their fears, and no culture to replace their anomie."[85]

Ouch. This "lost" generation grew up with divorce (not a new concept, but not practiced so freely until this generation), Nixon's dishonesty, and the rise of the yuppie. It's no wonder they were suspicious of "the man" and unwilling to commit to years of service to one company like their parents did.

This information describes Generation X before today. Perhaps in their twenties, some individuals in Generation X were disillusioned and disoriented, but the workforce today is in the prime of their career lifespan. Over half of executives believe Generation X is the generation that's most invested in their jobs.[86] They're at the point in their careers where they have the experience to back up their knowledge and still enough years before retirement to advance, spark innovation, and help guide the younger generations up the leadership pipeline.

Members of Generation X are motivated to stay in their jobs by money, their ability to make a difference in their organization, financial stability, and a sense of pride in their work. Only 16 percent are motivated to retain their employment because of job stability, while 48 percent think pay and bonuses are the most important benefit a job can offer.[87] They find their impact on the organization equally as important, though.

Further, members of Generation X are independent. They don't want to be micromanaged. This generation is sometimes referred to as the latch-key generation because they experienced more time alone than any previous generation. While their mothers were joining the rat race in large numbers, and their workaholic fathers were gone most of the time, Generation X was learning self-sufficiency.

The relationship between technology and Generation X is interesting. They were the generation of the Atari, the first microcomputers, pagers, and mobile phones, so technology isn't elusive to them. They brought in the technology age, saw it grow, become an independent form, and then transform at a rapid pace. Only 31 percent of Generation X say that technology makes their lives easier, compared to 74 percent of millennials.[88]

The "lost" generation is anything but. They're a group of independent thinkers who ushered innovation into the world for the masses to consume. This generation is poised as the backbone of the workplace, an integral, stable group with heaps of experience that accepts tech as a powerful tool and is ready for the retirement boom of baby boomers so they can step into their rightful place as leaders. They judge success based on what they can do for a company and the sense of pride they get from their work.

Millennials

Millennials dominate conversations about satisfying the current workforce, innovation, and markers for success. Also known as Generation Y or the Me Generation, millennials *are* the current conversation. The reason millennials control so much of the thought process behind workplace dynamics is because they'll make up 75 percent of the workforce within the next ten years.[89]

Millennials get a bad rap, though. If you believe the internet, they've killed everything, or are in the process of killing everything. It's said that millennials are entitled, self-absorbed, and unwilling to work hard for what they want. Another accusation against millennials is that they're disloyal to employers. This one perhaps has a bit of merit. In a 2016 survey of millennials in the workplace, Deloitte found 66 percent of millennials expect to leave their job before 2020.[90]

That same study found the likely reason for the disloyalty was a deficit in the company's use and enhancement of millennials' skills. In other words, millennials feel neglected. Only 28 percent of millennials feel the full offering of their skills are being used. The study further found millennials prioritize good pay, generating and supporting jobs, and providing a service or goods that make a positive difference in people's lives as their highest motivators in working for a company.

As tech babies who grew up with Oregon Trail on DOS, the rapid change from Nintendo to Super Nintendo to Wii to computer-like consoles such as Xbox One, and ten generations of iPhones, millennials depend on technology in their everyday lives. They expect a company to provide technology because they believe its the most efficient way to complete their tasks. And when a technology no longer serves its function, they look for the next best thing to do the job.

Despite the idea that millennials are a self-absorbed, reality TV–watching group of individuals out of touch with traditional life experiences, the statistics say differently. Most millennials desire a good work/life balance, a partner, a home, and financial security. In fact, the top five factors that influence a millennial's job choice are:

1. Good work/life balance
2. Opportunities to progress and be leaders
3. Flexible hours and the ability to work remotely
4. Sense of meaning from their work
5. Professional development training programs

The biggest takeaway here is that millennials value freedom. They consider some traditional markers (home, pay, and family) for success, but they're willing to sacrifice ideas of over-the-top financial success (owning a vacation house, for example) to be happy at work. As Sarah Landrum writes in her article, "How Millennials Are Changing How We View Success," "Success isn't the driving force here—it's a consequence. Millennials are teaching us nothing more or less than that we shouldn't be unhappy at work. And if we are, we owe ourselves something better."[91]

Generation Z

Most conversations center around Generation X and millennials, but it's a mistake to exclude Generation Z's voice when discussing success, especially since they're the future of our workforce. The oldest members of Generation Z, born around 1995, are in their early twenties and preparing to graduate college or already in the workforce. The negative discussion surrounding Generation Z is that this is a tech-obsessed group of kids glued to their phones with no idea how to function should digitization suddenly come to an end.

Though there's a kernel of truth to that, this generation is driving what our futures will look like. Some statistics surrounding Generation Z and their ideas about work are worth noting. For example, 62 percent of Generation Z anticipate challenges working with baby boomers and Generation X, while only 5 percent anticipate challenges working with millennials.[92] While baby boomers will retire out of the workforce in the coming years, Generation X and Generation Z will need to find a way to work together.

One thing that may unite them are their ideals surrounding success. The number one workplace motivation for Generation Z are opportunities for advancement. Similar to Generation X, Generation Z wants career advancement and more money (the second-highest motivator). The gap between the two groups may be how they view technology, and how their views of technology affect their views of each other.

Generation X uses tech to enhance their lives, but they're not native to it. In contrast, technology is an integral, natural part of Generation Z's lives. Two in three think anything is possible because of technology, while nine in ten would hate to give up their internet connection.[93] This doesn't mean they value technology over everything else, though. In fact, 51 percent prefer in-person communication with managers over email or instant messaging.

Though Generation Z anticipates problems with Generation X, they actually have more in common with them than they think. Most believe they'll have to work hard for what they want (77 percent), one-third want to become managers within five years of entering the workforce, and 79 percent want to work at mid- to large-size organizations.[94] The primary reason for the similarities between Generation X and Generation Z is that most of Generation Z are the children of Generation X.

They saw the recession and their parents struggle during that time. They learned that hard work was necessary to stay afloat during crises, so they're entering the workforce less entitled than millennials, who were raised in a world that was relatively financially stable, did. Raised by Generation X and the financial insecurity the recession brought, it's no wonder 60 percent of Generation Z sees money as a marker of success. Unlike previous generations, though, Generation Z sees value in making an impact. They want their jobs to mean something. They volunteer. They want to advance their goals through education, and during their free time, they want to be productive and creative.

Generation Z is still young. What they'll do remains to be seen, but we do know they're prepared to step out from the shadows of the baby boomers, Generation X, and millennials whose preoccupation with entitlement, financial distress, and arguments over tech usage have had incredible influence on how Generation Z defines its own success.

Cross-Generational Themes of Success

Wages. Fulfillment. Innovation: These three keywords show up in each generation's list of motivators. The metrics used to determine how they affect the idea of success for the generation is usually different, but the predominant theme remains.

Wages

Generation X values pay and bonuses, but not as incentives to do their jobs. They want good pay and bonuses as evidence they're doing well.

Millennials value wages that fit their experience and skills. But given the choice between high pay and no life outside of work or lower pay and flexibility, they'll choose the latter.

Generation Z wants money. They've lived through the effects of financial distress, and they don't want to experience it again. They want the company they work for to show a greater concern for global problems. They don't want a corporation that will simply chuck dough at them without global responsibility.

Fulfillment

Giving is important for Generation X. They want to give their skills and time to their companies, and they pride themselves on these unselfish acts.

Millennials value personal fulfillment, including at the workplace. They want their employers to offer benefit packages that allow them to pursue life outside of work. Instead of living to work, they want to work to live.

Environmental and social responsibility are big for Generation Z. They want career fulfillment in companies that care about the world, not just themselves.

Innovation

All three generations are techies. Technology has been an integral part of their daily lives for so long, they may struggle if the digital world suddenly ceased to exist.

As leaders or prospective leaders of industry, Generation X looks for ways to augment and advance business operations.

Millennials want innovative options that make their jobs more efficient and straightforward. They don't want to mess around with complicated processes or convoluted methods.

Generation Z wants a happy medium between technological advancement and personal approaches to management. For them, the best workplace combines innovation and individualism.

Output or Input?

Understanding the motivations for the generations in the digital age and how they define success are key factors in determining whether a business should value input or output. It also helps you determine what type of business you want to work for, because a company shows where its values and priorities lie when it chooses between input and output.[95]

Inputs drive outputs, but they can be one-sided. For example, a company may track the volume of sales calls and reward high call numbers (input) because it believes the more people it reaches, the higher the probability of a sale taking place. Output is outcome-oriented. While the company focuses on the volume of calls, what it really needs is the sales (output). It thinks that by controlling the input, it'll increase output, but this focus can cause disillusionment among the sales team as they begin to think of themselves more as dialing robots than individuals who are working toward results.

If it sounds like you need an even balance between input and output, you likely already know that the two must coexist in some way. What's important here is asking a high-value question, such as, "Do I want to work for a company that values input over output?" or "Does this promotion I want meet my input versus output preferences?"

In a nutshell: input in synonymous with behaviors and output equals results.[96] Cases can be made for both input- and output-driven positions, and your generation may affect which you prefer.

Freedom-loving millennials will value output-driven positions that allow them the autonomy to decide how to get results. On the other hand, Generation X and Generation Z may prioritize the rewards of input positions where their ritualistic behaviors will be comfortable with the process, and when the process no longer works, their innovation-obsessed natures will seek solutions that drive greater output.

In the digital age, success has similar meanings to the different generations, but getting to that point is a bit different for each. We've analyzed how the generations react in the workplace, what motivates each group, and how those motivators can affect whether the group thrives in process or freedom.

These are mostly generalizations based on statistics. Some individuals in each group may feel like they belong more to another group than their own, and that's okay. What's important here is that you ask yourself the high-value questions that will lead to greater awareness of what niche you fit in and how you can find greater success in your career by considering what you actually want.

What's My Place in the Workforce of the Future?

Once you know what you want, you can begin to question what your place in the workforce and how your career will develop in the workforce of the future. Generation Z is just starting out and Generation X still has fifteen to thirty working years left. Though the baby boomers are starting to retire, the rest of the workforce is still young and primed to bring the three things they value as success factors into the future.

Several studies have investigated the forces that will shape the future. These studies discuss the workforce broadly, but it's also helpful to analyze the data from a personal view. This is part of Questioneering. Ask the high-value questions, then find the high-value answers. Through this process, you can find your place in the future and understand how your career may develop as you advance. Four key questions will aid you as you consider opportunities ahead of you:

1. What megatrends will shape my future workforce?
2. How can workplace flexibility drive my career development?
3. How can I facilitate innovation at my job?

4. How will furthering individualism affect my goals and success markers?

As you continue to define success and what you want out of life, you'll be faced with these questions repeatedly. Individualism, innovation, flexibility, and the shaping forces of the future workforce are factors that enhance career fulfillment and will affect what path you choose to take as you seek high-value answers.

What Megatrends Will Shape My Future Workforce?

PwC completed a significant study on the workforce of the future. Their analytics speak to the outlook for 2030 and how the forces today are shaping the time ahead. The report discusses megatrends—the economic, social, political, and business dynamics that are gaining momentum to affect change. In the broader picture, these are sweeping transformations that will revolutionize business from the top down.

And that affects you.

According to the PwC study, your ambition, motivation, and success will be shaped by these five megatrends:

1. Technological breakthroughs
2. Demographic shifts
3. Rapid urbanization
4. Shifts in global economic power
5. Resource scarcity and climate change[97]

Technological Breakthroughs

The workforce today shares its space with automation and AI. As innovation improves upon previous versions of these technologies, the workers will find tech will be increasingly prevalent. PwC says, "Technology has the power to improve our lives, raising productivity, living standards and average lifespan, and free people to focus on personal fulfillment. But it also brings the threat of social unrest and political upheaval if economic advantages are not shared equitably."[98] Breakthroughs in technology will be a large part of your success as you decide which jobs will utilize your expertise and which promotions may require additional education to take.

Demographic Shifts

A large part of this shift is the aging baby boomer generation, whose exit from the workforce will signal a greater need for innovative employee options. There simply aren't enough workers moving into the workforce to make up for their exit. PwC explains, "The shortage of a human workforce in a number of rapidly aging economies will drive the need for automation and productivity enhancements.... Our longer life span will affect business models, talent ambitions and pension costs."[99] Businesses must adapt to the smaller labor population in a world that demands no slowdown in productivity. Your place in the workforce will be greater than ever, and your long-term goals may be affected by a labor market that needs your knowledge and proficiency longer than you expected.

Rapid Urbanization

PwC offers two important statistics that show rapid urbanization as a megatrend, "By 2030, the UN projects that 4.9 billion people will be urban dwellers and, by 2050, the world's urban population will have increased by some 72 percent."[100] They further explain that this affects the workforce because cities will become important hubs for job creation. Where do you live? What jobs are available in your area? These questions are important to consider as you think about your future in the workforce. Does your career development include a move to a new location? If not, are there enough advancement opportunities to help you achieve the balance of personal and career fulfillment in your area?

Shifts in Economic Power

Developing and developed nations alike have everything to gain and everything to lose. Globalization will arrive at your front door and have far-reaching effects on the future of labor in your country. PwC says, "Rapidly developing nations, particularly those with a large working-age population, that embrace a business ethos, attract investment and improve their education system will gain the most.... [While] the erosion of the middle class, wealth disparity and job losses due to large-scale automation will increase the risk of social unrest in developed countries."[101] Though you may not have a path to affect economic change on a grand scale, accounting for the shift of financial power and preparing yourself with education and training to attain desired skillsets will be more important than ever for your career development.

Resource Scarcity and Climate Change

The trend in green business practices will only grow as humanity seeks to find ways to live in the world without destroying it. Threats of resource scarcity and climate change could have devastating effects on life and have created the need for advanced technology that can power our lives. PwC predicts, "New types of jobs in alternative energy, new engineering processes, product design and waste management and re-use will need to be created to deal with [the] demand for energy and water [which] is forecast to increase by as much as 50 percent and 40 percent respectively by 2030."[102]

Expect traditional resource jobs to be restructured while alternative energy companies become top energy suppliers. This is another area where innovation will be king. Understanding how your skills fit in the alternative energy puzzle can unlock potential career development opportunities you may not have considered without asking the high-value question, *What megatrends are shaping my place in the future of the workforce?*

How Can Workplace Flexibility Drive My Career Development?

You can barely read an article or book on workplace trends without finding something about flexibility. In fact, so popular is this trend that it forced companies to consider and offer unconventional options to office work. Research done by WorldatWork and FlexJobs showed that "the majority of companies surveyed (80 percent) offer flexible work arrangements to employees."[103] The top three flexibility options—telework on an ad hoc basis, flex time, and part-time schedules—show employers aren't entirely committed to the top flexibility trends. The top trends suggest an uptick in interest for digital nomads, virtual companies, the gig economy, and better training for managers overseeing virtual workforces.

Digital Nomads

Technology brought the world together. More than in any other time, people feel like global citizens. Exploring the world has greater availability to the general population, and people want the freedom to take their work and go. To be a digital nomad, an employee must have a mostly virtual job and understand modern communication tech. Digital nomads have a leg up on those who stay put, as they network and discover opportunities worldwide.

Virtual Companies

No office. No commute. Totally cyberconnected. Virtual companies are so called because they exist away from the traditional brick-and-mortar structure. They don't pay rent or utilities. Instead, they can employ workers from any location, in any time zone, and all functions take place online. Like digital nomads, virtual companies require employees who can communicate proficiently through web services such as Slack, Skype, and Google Hangouts.

A study by FlexJobs showed that in 2014 only twenty-six companies were entirely virtual. By 2016, that number had risen to 125.[104] This reflects a 380 percent growth in virtual companies in just two years. There are industries that will never be virtual, but it's an important trend to consider when you think about how flexibility can drive your development, as there are certain skillsets that you need to work in this truly flexible career path.

Gig Economy

The gig economy is a haven for creatives—designers, writers, programmers, and artists are all used to the concept of freelancing. This field has expanded in recent years and is no longer just the starving artist's modus operandi; it's a viable alternative to traditional employment. Consultants, mechanics, engineers, and others freelance to supplement their income or entirely rely on projects to financially survive.

Freelancing gives the worker control. You can pick what projects to take on, what schedule you'll abide by, and as a by-product, the amount of money you want to make. Have a slow social schedule this week? Take on more work. Need next Wednesday off to go to the opening of a new museum? No problem. Freelancing promises a balance between personal and career fulfillment by allowing you to decide when you work. The drawback to freelancing is that you're at the mercy of available projects and, at the start, it can be difficult to build up a stable of clients that trust you to deliver. This trend provides the ultimate flexible work situation, but it can also enhance career development. As you seek promotions, you can learn something from freelancing—offering your higher-level services to gain experience before applying for the job at work.

Manager Training

With advancing free workforce platforms in play, managers are more important than ever. Digital nomads, freelancers, and virtual companies often rely on project managers and management teams to oversee the employee and perform quality-control checks on completed work.

Unfortunately, the WorldatWork and FlexJobs study found 86 percent of managers lack training on how to manage flexible employees. Keeping free-roaming employees motivated and focused can be tricky, and communication over text can present complications. It's imperative that managers are properly trained to provide the best value to the company.

Perhaps your area of expertise is in management. It's time to consider how virtual workforces will affect your job, and what training you can get to enhance your skills to appropriately handle these individuals. The trend toward flexibility in the workplace can play a role in your career development, especially when the balance between personal and career life is more important than ever. It's time to ask the high-value question, *How can workplace flexibility drive my career development?* Then look to the trends for answers.

How Can I Facilitate Innovation at My Job?

PwC's study discusses the world of innovation first. They suggest that when innovation becomes the primary focus, few rules exist. Speed takes over as the key to solutions. It says that workers will find that, "specialism is highly prized in the Red World [of innovation] and a career, rather than being defined by an employer or institution, is built from individual blocks of skills, experience and networks."[105]

In this world, highly skilled workers will be valuable, but laggards will find themselves left out of gainful employment. If PwC is correct and innovation is a megatrend that will change the future of the workforce, it seems necessary to consider the high-value question, *How can I facilitate innovation at my job?*

You're the rod that attracts the lightning bolt. You know your job. You've spent time studying the industry, memorizing policies and procedures, and becoming an expert in your field, but your industry doesn't owe you anything, and organizations have a plethora of talent at their fingertips. You have an opportunity to accelerate and ease innovation as it comes to your workplace—the harbinger of change and the facilitator that encourages acceptance of it.

How many times have you listened to employees or colleagues complain because the procedure they were used to changed, and they didn't like it? The truth is, they weren't used to it. Liking something and being used to it are two different things.

If I teach my daughter to drive with both feet, when I ask her to change to only one foot, she won't like it. She'll say it doesn't feel natural, and it makes no sense for me to ask such a ridiculous thing. But the truth is, two-footed driving can result in accidents if the driver mistakenly presses the wrong pedal in an emergency situation. While two-footed driving used to be necessary for compressing a clutch on manual vehicles, cars with automatic transmissions provide an innovative alternative to two-footed driving. Of course, with a manual transmission, the second foot goes on the clutch, not the brake, so it's not a dangerous situation. But with two-footed driving in an automatic, one foot is on the gas and one on the brake, which can lead to left-right issues when the brain freezes in panic. So, we discovered it was unnecessary to use two feet, and it was, in fact safer. But when I tell her she has to make the change, even if I explain why the change is important, she will still have the instinctual urge to fight it.

That's human nature. We don't appreciate or accept change at first. And the really crazy thing is, once we do accept the change and adapt to it, if we go back to the old way or progress to a new way, we get just as upset as when we had to make the initial change. This is why we need facilitators of innovation. This is where you come into play. You must consider what value you have to offer your company as an implementer, organizer, or architect of the innovation they need.

Perhaps there's a process that can be expedited or a sales program that's outdated and you know of a program that will save money and enhance operations. Share the idea! If your company implements a new software, become an advocate for it. Learn it with the excitement of a child with a new toy, and maybe offer to become a trainer once you're comfortable with it.

Knowing how you can facilitate the advancement of innovation within your company is a key factor in achieving your career development goals. When an employer sees you as a champion of the company, they'll be more likely to trust you and to want to see you in higher positions within the organization.

How Will Furthering Individualism Affect My Goals and Success Markers?

Individualism is a philosophy igniting change in business and driving trends across the globe. It focuses on the individual and his or her worth as a person and promotes the idea that people should have the right to pursue self-realization. With the generational focus on personal happiness as a marker for success, it's no wonder individualism has taken hold in the workforce.

We can see the individualistic approach in trends, such as workplace flexibility where employees ask employers to fit work to their lifestyles. Individualism also focuses on morality and the responsibility of each person to show their moral worth. This is shown in PwC's research and predictions for the workforce of the future. "Workers find flexibility, autonomy and fulfillment, working for organizations with a strong social and ethical record. This is the collective response to business fragmentation; the desire to do good, for the common good," the study says.[106]

If any of this sounds familiar, it's because the attitude toward honest, honorable work is a primary value of the majority of Generation X, millennials, and Generation Z. As the future of the workforce, their values must take priority for companies if they want to attract and retain talent.

PwC predicts collaboration, transparency, fluidity, and digital platforms as four key drivers of individualism in the future workforce, and these drivers should be considered when you ask the high-value question, *How will furthering individualism affect my goals and success markers?*

As the workforce becomes more collaborative, you may find that your own goals are directly affected by other individuals. Understanding how to effectively use partnerships and professional relationships becomes an important aspect of your career development. Greater transparency in the business will also benefit you as you set your goals. The information you can garner from transparent managers and executives will help you judge what additional skills or training you may need to progress.

You're the future of the workforce. Define your place in that future. Ask yourself how the megatrends—innovation, flexibility, and individualism—can help you develop your career and achieve your goals and provide high-value answers that will further aid you in finding fulfillment in your personal life.

What Questions Should I Ask During Interviews?

Interviewing is an art form. Knowing what to say, when to say it, and how to present yourself can make or break your ability to get the job. Even if you're the most highly skilled and most experienced person, real top talent, if you botch the interview, you may miss out on an opportunity to advance your career.

There's a plethora of information available online, from coaching to sample questions, to aid you in refining your approach to interviews. The high-value question that can really enhance your experience in interviews is, *What questions should I be asking during interviews?*

Asking questions during an interview help you gain valuable insight into the day-to-day duties of the job. High-value questions enable you to better understand the expectations of the position. Asking questions also offers your interviewer more insights into your skillset.

The process of asking questions during an interview is called due diligence.

Doing your due diligence before you take a job is an important part of avoiding a position that may stall your career or take away from your sense of fulfillment. So, try not to let your nerves get the best of you and ask these six vital, high-value questions in every job interview:

1. By what metrics is the person in this position measured?
2. Who are the other individuals in my department and customer base and how will I interact with them?
3. What technology does the person in this position use?
4. What do the company's executives care most about and what are they like?
5. What potential added responsibilities and upward mobility may this position experience?
6. Can you tell me the thirty-sixty-ninety-day plan for this job? What are the most important accomplishments within that period?

These high-value questions offer you the potential to learn about the company culture, the company's use of tools of innovation, and the expectations of the job that could impact your fulfillment within the position.

Revamping Your Digital Persona

If you're not already honing your online presence, you need to start now. With more than 3.2 billion internet users and millions of businesses creating their digital personas, not being online is setting you back. From business professional networking sites such as LinkedIn to the numerous job listings sites, opportunities abound. Your digital persona is your brand. It's the thing people judge you by. The first thing you need to consider is whether you even like your digital persona. If you don't like it, how will others, like potential employers, take to it?

Your digital persona should be a second you. A separate you, it should encompass all the positive traits you offer the world. Mars Dorian, a digital illustrator and storyteller who helps people stand out online, says, "Your real self is stuffed with doubts and problems carried over from society. When that confused self goes online, it's still acting in a similar way. Instead of treating the online world like a blank new slate, you'll carry your garbage from the real world and thus neglect your *awesome* creative abilities. But if you look at your online self as a new opportunity, you'll see how much potential you have access to."[107] If you're just starting out with a new digital persona or considering rebranding yourself, there are a few steps you can take to portray a stronger online character, and these steps are the same steps top businesses use when they enter the online world.

Write an Overview

An effective summary reflects your personality in bite-sized, easily digestible chunks. Consider the top four adjectives you want people to associate with you. Really dig deep into your creativity to draft descriptions around those words to showcase the truth about who you are. LinkedInsights.com suggests avoiding buzzwords and clichés, including these most-used words: strategic, organizational, motivated, driven, passionate, track record, responsible, extensive experience, dynamic, and creative.[108]

Choose Your Values

Identifying your principles will help you decide what type of a person you want to present to the outside world. Using your four adjectives from your overview, add to or take away from them to define a set of three to five values that are most important for people to take away from your digital persona, for example:

1. Honest, dependable, timely
2. Innovative thinking that leads to breakthrough insights
3. Output-oriented, entrepreneurial, independent-thinker

Define Your Voice

Your writing style is your online voice. As most anyone who has ever had a sarcastic text misconstrued can tell you, digital communication is tough. People who read your blogs, tweets, or posts must have a clear understanding of what you're trying to convey. Consider the following examples:

1. I always tell people they need to get onboard or get out of the way. There's no reason for smart people to resist innovation and change.

2. Innovation is a bulldozer driving through old procedures and processes. It can seem difficult to keep up, but facilitating the changes will help you advance your skillset and maybe even your career!

One of these communications is negatively slanted and can be misconstrued as elitist or insulting. The other acknowledges the feelings of the audience and helps them see what a powerful role they could play in bringing about change in their industry. How you say things matters. So, spend some time writing and allow people you trust to review what you've written for areas of improvement. And whatever you do, don't tweet when you're mad!

Digital Exhaust

Speaking of things you should avoid on the internet, the new term *digital exhaust* is making waves. It's an important term to familiarize yourself with. Digital exhaust is data produced from regular online activities. Whenever you're online, whether you're surfing the web, doing research, or checking social media, you're delivering data to servers about who you are, what you want, and how to sell to you.

Avoiding digital exhaust may seem impossible, but through managed attribution, you can control your digital persona. Managed attribution is "the ability to control the appearance of your internet persona and how activities are linked back to you."[109] Managed attribution is discussed at corporations that want to protect their brand and avoid cyber criminals. Several online products help with this. You may not need something as extreme as false location services, but it's important to be aware of the trail you're leaving on the internet and ways to manage it. Your managed attribution strategy may include not using public computers or servers or using private browsing sessions when switching between your public and private personas.

Your digital persona is important, and in the future, it will play a larger role in advancing your career. Managing your persona and finding ways to control your digital exhaust should be top short-term priorities. How you present yourself on the web may be the first impression a potential employer has of you, and first impressions are everything.

What Insights Can I Gain by Comparing My Personal Management with Top Company Management?

So, you understand how your goals and personal fulfillment are affected by generational values, you've figured out your place in the future workforce, and you've learned to manage your digital persona, but all of that will mean nothing if you don't have a handle on personal management. You can gain many insights by looking at the top companies and applying some of their business models to your own personal life.

Running your personal management like a top company—with spending plans, relationship building, and time management—can keep you organized, productive, and fiscally responsible.

Business Plans for Spending

Smart businesses have a spending plan. A spending plan is an "aggregate budget composed of departmental or individual budgets for an accounting period, program, or project."[110] In other words, companies don't lump all their money into one account and then try to figure out where to send it and whom to pay. They break their accounts down into smaller, more manageable departments with their own budgets.

Your personal finances could take a page from that book. Budgeting is instrumental to financial success, and once you've created and used your budget, you'll be able to incorporate other business ideas such as budget forecasting and future planning. The abundance of money coaches online will tell you that through budget forecasting, you can predict what months money will be tight and when you'll have excess.

Spending plans in businesses are about projections. Knowing what your income will be in June or how it may rise around the holidays. You can apply the idea of projections to your own life. Doing so can help your career development.

Imagine you want to move to a digital nomad lifestyle within five years. If you're not freelancing and have a steady income, great! But different locations have different costs of living. Living expenses in Thailand are dwarfed by those in France. And if you plan on doing three months in one place and three in the other, it's important you can predict your lean months and how to manage the added outflow of the more expensive nation.

Alternately, you may be looking at freelancing as you roam the world. In that case, you'll need to know what months you have fewer clients, when you need to take on more work, and how to save the excess for the lean months.

Relationship Building

Our digital world has given us the opportunity to connect with people worldwide. But many people feel more alone than ever.[111] If we take a cue from business, we would find that managing our relationships is crucial to developing both personal and career success. It's no secret that an active social life and awesome networking skills will lead to greater fulfillment, so shying away from it is unhealthy, especially when maintaining these relationships are fairly easy to build and contain so much potential. Friends, family, clients, colleagues, and bosses can be your best allies when it comes to your personal development.

These relationships need nurturing. Consider how a business might nurture a relationship with a top client or partner, with lunch, golf, drinks, gifts, or meetings to exchange ideas and opportunities. These are all things you can apply to your own relationships to cultivate growth. Perhaps once a month you go to lunch with your contact in the IT department. Or every other Sunday, you meet up with a group of co-workers for bowling. What you do with people doesn't have to be constant, but it should be consistent.

If we can learn anything from how businesses foster relationships, it's that consistency is key. Think about the business whose goal is to be top-of-mind of its paper customers. As a paper supplier, it'll check on their customers regularly, offer upgraded products for new projects you've told them about, and find ways to incentivize your purchases. They will consistently provide you with care and support, or they'll lose your business.

The same can be applied to a more personal approach to relationships. If you're top-of-mind, your friends, family, and colleagues will think of you first when they hear of opportunities that might fit your skillset. Further, nurturing your relationships may lead to training or additional education that will advance your career.

Aside from all the career development opportunities, studies have shown the positive effects of social interactions and developing relationships on the psyche. Staving off depression, increasing your immune system and productivity, getting better sleep, and maintaining brain health are all tied to a vibrant social life.[112] To maximize your potential for career and personal fulfillment, don't pass up the opportunity to manage your relationships like companies manage their partnerships.

Time Management

There are only twenty-four hours in a day, and when you consider eight to twelve of those hours your are unconscious, traveling, eating, or helping your kids with homework, it can seem like the hours just keep dwindling and nothing ever gets accomplished. Effectively managing your time is a big factor in controlling your life like a business.

Peter F. Drucker of the Drucker Institute famously said, "Until we can manage time, we can manage nothing else."[113] You have so many demands placed on you throughout the day—hunger, paying attention to your children, work projects—it's imperative that you have the skills to put your ducks in a row if you have any hope of accomplishing anything at all. A few easy ways to more effectively manage your hours include:

1. **Make a List**: Keeping everything in your head is detrimental to your ability to realistically plan your day. Making a list or keeping a calendar of events, projects, and plans will keep you sane, even if you think you can remember it all. This goes beyond jotting down a reminder that your child has a soccer game on Saturday. Make lists or keep calendars of everything that takes up too much of brain space. Plan meals ahead of time so you aren't rushing around trying to decide what to have. Keep a calendar of deadlines for projects. Write down get-togethers with friends. If you have an idea, make a note of it. Don't risk losing the information or forgetting dates by trying to manage it all in your head.

2. **Get Up Earlier**: The wee hours of the morning can be the most productive. It's quiet. No one in the house is up yet. You have the space to think, and your brain is refreshed (hopefully!) from a good night's sleep. You haven't had the stressors of the day hit you yet, and the exhaustion you'll start to feel around 8 o'clock in the evening, when you've been weighed down all day, is a distant concern. Your brain works, and this is the time to use it. Further, you'll be forcing yourself into a routine that increases discipline. You may not want to get out of bed early every morning, but every small war you win over your mind is a step toward a life that you control. Top CEOs,

including Richard Branson and Mark Zuckerberg, are earlier risers and swear by the sunrise.

3. **Simplify Your Life**: How many extracurricular activities are your children in, and who is responsible for getting them there, dressed in the appropriate uniforms, and getting them home? How many outside demands are placed on you that don't offer you fulfillment in your career *or* life? How many derailed meetings are you sitting through when you could be using the time productively? Analyzing how busy your life is by asking those questions will change the way you think about doing things. You can take back control in some areas to end the frantic cycle of trying to do too much in too little time. Many of us push ourselves to the limit, but having downtime to think, mull over the day, or destress is crucial to success.

You can simplify your life purely by taking back control of your time. Be direct in meetings and speak with the boss about how much more productive you could be if the meetings were shortened. Be honest with your family about not being everything to all people. Let your kids do their own laundry. Ask your spouse to trade-off on shuttling your kids to their activities. It's okay to communicate the need for simplicity in your life, but it's equally important that you follow through on what you say.

So, simplify—simple as that.

The high-value questions you ask while Questioneering will lead to high-value answers, including those covered in this chapter:

1. How is success defined in the digital age?
2. What's my place in the workforce of the future?
3. What questions should I be asking during interviews?
4. How can I better manage my digital persona to increase my client base?

5. What insights can I gain by comparing my personal management with top company management?

Your clarity of purpose will drive your career development, and that starts with being honest with yourself and understanding how you define success, what you bring to the workforce of the future, and how you can better manage yourself and your digital persona.

Your personal happiness and career success are built upon the ability to critically analyze where you are and where you want to be. Questioneering isn't only for driving breakthrough innovation in business, but can lead to a powerful re-discovery of your human spirit. Here are QBAM frameworks for two questions we discussed this chapter.

Q	How can I better manage my digital persona?
B	My digital persona is the first impression many people get of me and it's a chance for me to put forward my most creative, confident self.
A	1. Choose the social media platforms most important to my digital persona. 2. Create a summary of myself that's not cliché. Define my values and voice so I can accurately project the image I want people to see. 3. Use available marketing tools to boost my readership or followers.
M	1. Achieve X number of page clicks/followers within the first six months. 2. Publish X number of tweets/blogs within the first six months.

Table 6: QBAM for Your Digital Persona

Q	How can I run my personal life like a top company runs their business?

B	I believe utilizing a spend plan, nurturing my relationships, and managing my time better can lead to a more fulfilling career and personal life.

	Utilizing a spend plan will direct my finances so I have more financial freedom and a better understanding of what's ahead of me financially.	Nurturing my relationships will lead to a more fulfilling life both personally and professionally.	Managing my time better will give me the opportunity to spend some time in thought, not live so frantically, and achieve more peace in my life.
A	1. Create a budget. 2. Use the budget for six months. 3. Using insight gained from the previous six months, forecast what the next three months will look like, and track how accurate my predictions are.	1. Establish a relationship with a colleague. 2. Reconnect with a friend or schedule a monthly outing with a friend. 3. Ask your boss for a one-on-one to gain insight into upward mobility and areas of improvement for your position.	1. Simplify the interactions and scheduling conflicts in my life. 2. Establish a routine for sleep. Make getting up early a priority. 3. Write everything down. Make grocery lists and food prep plans. Carry a calendar and notebook to write down appointments and ideas right away.
M	1. Save X number of dollars within the first six months. 2. Achieve accurate forecasting.	1. Have at least a monthly plan to hang out with friend and go to lunch with colleague. 2. A prepared list of insights on work performance and areas of improvement.	1. Get up at scheduled time every day for one month. 2. Have moved all scheduling notes to calendar within first two weeks of plan.

Table 7: QBAM for Your Personal Life

In our final discussion about Questioneering, we'll cover the core subject of technology itself. We'll tackle the Answer Mindset head on and discuss the angst surrounding technological development today—the defining generational game-changer of our time. As with any change we fear, it will be our responsibility to try to do a better job of understanding technology. To take that step, we first need to understand its current context and the unfounded fears that surround technology today. Often, these fears translate into low-value questions. So, let's investigate the questions we ask about technology so we can unpack the misconceptions and correct our understanding, with the ultimate goal of asking the high-value question.

CHAPTER FIFTEEN

Will Technology Uplift or Replace the Human Spirit?

THE EMERGENCE OF DIGITAL culture is clearly a formative moment for human society. In the space of a few decades—a comparatively miniscule amount of time—technology has fundamentally altered the way we create, process, spread, and store information. The results will have a profound impact on how humans interact, and indeed, on what humans are even capable of. This is what we refer to as the intersection of digital culture and humanism. It's a place where two seemingly distinct, different, and historically disparate ideas come together. So, let's investigate the concepts of digital culture and humanism.

I Am a Digital Humanist: Synthesis of Digital Culture and Humanism

The history of humanism suggests parallels to the current day. Humanism was born during the Renaissance, itself a time of rebirth, as the name of the era means in its original French. We understand the Renaissance today as a period characterized by celebration of the human spirit, and everything it means to be human. It was a golden age of music, art, invention, and literature, of de' Medici and da Vinci, Michelangelo and Raphael, Shakespeare and Petrarch. Cultural icons of this era came to define much of European history, and our ideas of European culture today are in many ways shaped by developments of the era.

What enabled the Renaissance and its confluence of information and culture to take place? None of it would have been possible without the printing press: a black swan of a technological development, a relatively simple piece of technology that changed everything. Guttenberg's innovation facilitated the spread of information in unprecedented ways, at formerly impossible rates, and with unimaginable consequences. Distilled to its essence, it was *information* that caused the Renaissance to happen. Access to information, and the ability to spread it quickly and efficiently led the natural desire and human instinct to create information in new and brilliant ways, in the form of what we recognize today as art, literature, and science that lifted a continent out of the dark ages and defined an era. The parallels between the Renaissance and the information age are evident, and the modern implications of applying new technology are virtually limitless. Viewed through the lens of humanism, the possibilities are endless: so, let's talk about humanism, a philosophy that itself originally emerged from technology.

Humanism is a school of ethics that focuses on the individual and is designed to elicit the very greatest of human potential and enshrine the worth of human values. The American Humanist Association describes humanism as a "rational philosophy informed by science, inspired by art, and motivated by compassion . . . affirming the dignity of each human being."[114] In its infancy during the Renaissance, the philosophy was driven by humans connecting with each other on a new level, enabled by their ability to communicate with each other thanks to the printing press.

Just as the printing press enabled the analog development of humanism, so too can modern technology cause its digital evolution. Digital communication is the modern equivalent of the printing press—a game-changing technology that has the potential to completely reframe the way humans interact with each other.

Before the Renaissance, only the highly educated had access to art and literature, and reading and writing were special abilities only certain people could afford and learn. It took years to master a craft so unique and specific that it was out of most people's reach. It's easy to think of digital technology in the same way. In the 1980s and 1990s, computers were highly specialized, and most people weren't familiar with how to interact with them, let alone program them. In the early 2000s, though computers and the internet were dramatically more accessible to the average person, web design, programming, and knowledge of hardware and software remained highly specialized, attainable largely by people willing to devote their careers or considerable time to mastering the science. Consider this time the digital dark age, pre-printing press.

Now, we're in the midst of a dramatic shift. The ability to learn about, interact with, and benefit from digital technology is no longer restricted to specialists and professionals. Digital technology and the incredible progress it enables is attainable by everybody. This is the result of a transition Martin Recke describes as moving "away from computer-literate people to people-literate technology."[115] The goal here isn't to make all people into digital and IT specialists. Instead, there's a trend towards making digital technology so simple and intuitive, the average person doesn't *need* to be a specialist. The technology is designed with the average user in mind, suited to them, and responsive to their needs.

I define myself as a Digital Humanist. I believe the purpose of technology is to unlock the hidden potential of the human spirit, not replace it. As an individual, entrepreneur, business leader, and human, I believe we must continue to ask the high-value questions and challenge a growing set of assumptions behind the warnings of our demise and way of life as humans as technologies advance. The Answer Mindset draws us to the superficial benefits of cost cutting, yet if we spend just a few minutes challenging our core assumptions, we'll unlock the benefits of increased value, job creation, and overall wellbeing. Let's dive deeper and challenge a few of these assumptions.

One of the chief concerns about the impact of technology on the world today is situated firmly in the economic sphere, but its consequences extend well into the social sphere, too. What consequences might automation have on the American economy? Often, the assumed answer is job loss. If that's true, what will the social effects of job loss be? We see here the negative results of framing a low-value question: a logical chain stems from the answer that seems itself to grow more and more negative. But reframe the question, and we find the potential for positive answers.

The negative assumptions about automation tend to follow a well-known path: technology is developing so quickly that it will replace humans, putting people out of a job, with far-reaching impacts on the economy. Beyond the economic effects, we hear fears about the social ills that could result. Imagine a generation of Americans without the manufacturing sector! Indeed, if it were true that automation would result in a jobless generation, the results would no doubt be catastrophic. But there's little real evidence to suggest that this might be the case, and a good deal of historical and contemporary evidence that tells us it probably isn't.[116]

Assumption: Machine Learning Will Displace Our Ability to Think

A cultural trope almost as old as the genre, a fear of machine learning occupies a space in the cultural consciousness, manifesting in science fiction and horror films. Books and films depicting dystopian or post-apocalyptic worlds in which machines have overthrown their creators span the information age. Even before the digital age began, authors such as Isaac Asimov wrote about human interactions with robots and artificial intelligence systems. Some science fiction stories are about friendships and working relationships with machines, other ones about societal dynamics. The *Terminator* series tells a terrifying story of the catastrophic results of machine learning, while films such as *I, Robot* take a more nuanced approach, examining the ethics and moral dynamics at play in a society where machine learning isn't only possible, but more advanced and ingrained in the culture than we might imagine. Entire philosophies have developed around the notion of the possibility of machine learning, perhaps best evidenced by Asimov's laws of robotics. Yet as exciting, scary, or dangerous as these fictional portrayals might be, they reflect neither the reality of machine learning, nor the ethical or human implications of it.

In books and movies, machine learning is a concrete thing, a discrete goal humans worked toward and eventually achieved with a variety of captivating fictional consequences. But this conceptualization of machine learning not only fails to reflect reality, it also fails to capture the essence of what machine learning really is and the goals it actually seeks to achieve.

Taking a Digital Humanist perspective, where humanism is the goal and digital culture is the context, we can understand the concept differently. Machine learning isn't an end in itself—there's no point in the future at which we might be able to say, "we've arrived!" Instead, it's an *approach* to development. Humans—researchers, developers, code writers, innovators—are always at the wheel, shaping the concept of machine learning even as it takes on a greater role in our lives. Where machines play a greater role in society, guided by their makers, they can have a tremendously beneficial and empowering effect on humans on an individual and societal level.

The key to understanding this distinction lies in the universal applicability of machine learning. This isn't a movie plotline come to life, in which artificial intelligence becomes sentient and pursues its own ends. Neither does reality truly reflect the way it's so often portrayed by cultural commentators, who paint a picture of technology as a runaway snowball, guided only by gravity and its own momentum, picking up size and speed, resisting human attempts to control it. Instead, viewing technological development through a humanist lens, we can understand technological development and machine learning has an *intensifying* effect, acting as a multiplier and a magnifier. It does not create, it acts upon things that have been created; it doesn't guide the hand of the inventor, it strengthens it. As MIT and Carnegie Mellon professors Erik Brynjolfsson and Tom Mitchell note, machine learning is "capable of accelerating the pace of automation itself . . . like the steam engine and electricity, [it] spawns a plethora of additional innovations and capabilities."[117] However, it does not itself act to create new innovations; rather, it's a powerful tool that allows the innovator even more license to create himself.

Here, we see the humanist approach coming into play. The value of humanism lies in empowering the individual. What greater empowerment can there be than unleashing the creative potential of the human spirit? By enabling ever greater innovation, machine learning advances the human cause of development by letting itself become engaged by humans in the task of creating—of being human.

Assumption: Technology Will Accelerate the Divide of Rich and Poor

A Core Belief of many detractors of technological development is the notion that it acts as a negative disrupter, a force that creates wealth only for those who develop it, own it, and control it. There are elements of many conflicting philosophies and worldviews in this approach: hints of Marxism, suggested by "controlling the means of development," and echoes of Goethe, who wrote in *Sorcerer's Apprentice* and even in *Faust* about the reality and consequences of hubristic approaches to technology.

My goal here isn't to label people fearful of technological progress as communists or Marxists or anything else, or even to suggest necessarily that those things are bad. They are worldviews and schools of thought. Even if we don't agree with them, that doesn't mean we shouldn't examine the role they play in shaping the way we think today. Like it or not (and some of us may indeed like it!), the ideas advanced by these worldviews are a part of the way we think about society and think critically about development.

Let's take Marxism as an example. To be clear, I'm not advocating or criticizing the viewpoint, I'm using it to try to explain the discourse surrounding the issues we're talking about, which is critical to understanding the issues themselves. A key tenant of Marxism has to do with class stratification, and that the technology created by the Industrial Revolution is responsible for inequalities in society because the wealthy own the technology that produces wealth, and therefore have leverage over the workers.

Technology and wealth, according to this way of thinking, lead to more advanced technology and ever greater wealth, creating a positive feedback loop, a vicious cycle in which the gap between rich and poor, owner and worker, and, in the context of the digital era, computer-literate and non-computer-literate, grows ever greater. This is the story Marxism tells, and we can see its natural parallel in some of the fears surrounding technological advancement. Due to the increasing rates of technological development, it often seems technology is advancing more quickly than we can learn to use it. The result, goes the argument, is that people who know how to control or use technology will have an advantage over those who don't, who don't have the time, resources, or interest to learn about how these complex new forces work. In the same way the Industrial Era led to the inequalities of the Gilded Age, Marxism argues the technology gap will perpetuate inequalities during the digital age.

Of course, we can also let history be our guide to understanding why this isn't true at all. Marxist theory predicts the inequalities created by development will eventually lead to a revolution, in which the lower class (the proletariat) overthrow the upper class (the bourgeoisie), or, in our parallel analogy, the users and creators of modern technology.

The problem with this theory? The revolution never took place. Where Communism did take hold, it was unsustainable and eventually broke down. And in the United States, where for a short period we did experience great inequality during the Gilded Age, we never even approached a revolution.

Instead, we used law and regulation to bridge the gap between rich and poor, breaking up monopolies and ensuring wealth couldn't just be handed down through dynasties and corporations. The result of this correction, and ultimately, the result also of the industrial technology Marxism feared, was a period, after World War II, of the greatest economic prosperity the United States had ever encountered. Living standards increased across the board, and the entire country, along with much of the world, became better off because instead of fearing and rejecting technological progress, they embraced it, harnessed it, and used it to improve the universal human condition. Obviously, that story isn't completely over, and there's work still to be done, but the story history tells us does suggest that technology isn't the disease, but the cure.

Let's apply this lesson to the digital era. A major concern is, for instance, that computer literacy will become the new means of production and the gap in knowledge between the computer-literate and illiterate will lead to a self-perpetuating hierarchy. But this claim takes a decidedly pessimistic view of the potential outcomes of technological development. Though the inner workings of machines and computers are increasingly complex, the machines and computers themselves don't necessarily become more complicated to use; indeed, the internal complexity is intended to serve an external simplicity. This trend has the ultimate effect of meaning that it doesn't *matter* if somebody doesn't know how to disassemble a microchip, they don't need to have advanced technological expertise, because the ultimate purpose is a simpler interface—technology that's easier, not harder, to use. The fundamental misunderstanding is that digital development doesn't lead to polarization, it leads to specialization, and that's a good thing.

Specialization means people can focus on their strengths and their interests, even their passions, without having to worry about keeping up in every other sector. Everybody wins. The phenomenon is known as competitive advantage, which refers to the idea that if everybody focuses on what they're best at, then everybody benefits. The computer technician creates the technology that allows the code writer to create the program that a geneticist uses to determine how to breed the most delicious apples that the farmer knows better than any of the others how to grow. Everybody specializes in their sector. Everybody makes a living. Everybody enjoys the apples.

In practical terms, this kind of equalization of knowledge resources is best captured by Martin Recke's phrase, the "shift away from computer-literate people to people-literate technology."[118] The focus shifts from the developers and to the users. The empowerment that follows—the same empowerment as was the result of the Industrial Revolution—is the realization of every individual's own ability, enhanced, magnified, and multiplied by technology.

This argument extends beyond individuals and can also be true for countries. Some of the same conceptions of technology's effect on society are at work when we think about the global effects of digital development as well. The concept of stratification between classes—the same story about self-perpetuating hierarchy, best examined through the lens of Marxism, also exist in another dimension—the international dimension, where stratification doesn't exist between classes, but instead, between countries.

The story, in its essence, goes that because modern technology was first developed in the Western world, the Western world will always retain the advantage of the best technology, which will perpetuate the difference between the west and the rest. There are many names for and many versions of this story, which all play out generally along the same lines.

In economic circles, this idea is known as *dependency theory*. In the same way that Marxism is an attempt to contextualize and understand the relationships between classes, dependency theory is an attempt to contextualize and understand the international system, mostly in economic terms. And in the same way I neither advocated for or detracted from Marxism as a philosophy, in this discussion, I don't assert that dependency theory is either correct or incorrect. It's just a way of looking at relationships so we can better understand them. It's a lens we can apply and remove, through which we can view the world, but it isn't necessarily the way we think the world is. In this case, it's a useful way to understand and explain an argument and to illustrate why that argument may not be valid.

The theory has a good deal in common with Marxism. It originally stems from Marxist theory, and the relationship will probably be fairly clear. Dependency theory posits that countries in the world are categorized into two broad groups: the periphery and the core. There are more complex and detailed iterations of this argument, including semi-peripheries and other nuanced relationships, but here it's enough just to paint in broad strokes.

The core consists of developed Western countries, wealthy nations that already have access to the most developed technology, resources, and markets. The core uses its wealth to buy natural resources such as oil, metals, and minerals from the periphery, as well as finished products that are manufactured in the periphery. Because the core countries are already wealthier, they can continue to pay for cheap labor in the periphery and buy finished products people living in the periphery cannot afford themselves. Consider, for example, that somebody working in a factory that manufactures computers may not be able to afford to buy a computer themselves.

Developed countries in the core use the finished products, resources, and technology they import from the periphery to develop even further, and the level of their technology continues to advance. Through this exchange, resources and technology do drift back into the periphery, but these countries theoretically will never have technology *as advanced* as the countries in the core do, because the core countries have the wealth and the knowledge always to stay on the cutting edge, and the periphery countries therefore develop more slowly.

Though dependency theory has historically been used to explain economic inequality on a broad, global scale, it has begun to take on the new form of explaining technological disparity—that because technology develops more quickly in wealthy countries that have the resources to devote to research, design, and development, poorer countries will never catch up, since technological progress in the digital age *enables* further, faster technological progress. But just as economic dependency theory began to lose credibility due to greater examination, so too does our technological dependency theory when we apply greater scrutiny.

It may be true up to a certain point, that technology will help core countries in the west more quickly than poorer countries in the periphery. A desktop computer is only as reliable as the power grid you plug it into, and a car is only as good as the road you're driving on. In the twentieth century, improved technology could not always compensate for the economic and infrastructural challenges poorer, less developed countries often faced.

However, as technological implications and consequences progress beyond the mechanical and into the digital, this no longer always holds true. We need look no further than the internet. In a digital environment, infrastructure remains relevant, but it lacks the same importance it once had. Going online provides the same power anywhere in the world. In rich countries and poor ones, everybody has access to the same internet. And as more and more technological development occurs in digital form, *access* to that knowledge can take place just as easily in Nairobi as it does in New York. Going online and sharing information digitally means the same thing regardless of where in the world you are. It affirms the value of the individual and the importance of universal human empowerment, irrespective of location, heritage, or home: a crucial element of humanism in the digital age.[119]

Assumption: Technology Will Advance Faster Than We Can Regulate, Causing Irreversible Societal Impacts

A genuine worry of those concerned about rapid technological advancement is the disparity between the rates of technological progress and the ability of regulators to respond to them. Regulations that lag behind development have the potential to be a real problem, but examined from another angle, it's clear the potential answers to this question lie in the very same patterns of growth that give rise to it.

Regulatory bodies are historically known for their comparatively sluggish responses to technological innovation. After all, it's necessary to fully understand a piece of technology, a concept, or a principle to regulate it. By the same token, regulators cannot leverage technology to improve regulatory ability without knowing how best to use that technology in the first place. By reframing this concern as a high-value question, we can gain better insight into answers that can have a profound positive impact.

Instead of asking, *How will technology likely make regulation more difficult?* we ought to ask, *What's the potential for technology to lend itself to regulation? And if we achieve that, how can we use it to benefit society?* Just because technology continues to develop, it does not necessarily become more complicated or harder to understand. Indeed, a major tech trend is towards simpler, more responsive, easier-to-use technologies and interfaces, even as the power behind them increases, too. Regulation can and should be a prominent issue as technology continues to evolve, and it can be put to positive use.

The finance sector has changed most dynamically due to technological development, though largely outside popular debates and conversations. Computing speed allows thousands of trades to take place around the world virtually instantaneously, something the founders of Wall Street wouldn't have thought possible. Contrary to the worries produced by a low-value question approach to regulatory issues, regulation itself has not slowed down the finance sector as technology has developed—quite the opposite. As the international banking group BBVA notes, the last decade has seen an enormous *increase* in regulation.[120] Far from indicating regulators' inability to keep up with the pace of change, empirical evidence suggests regulators are responding to the pace of change with bureaucratic enthusiasm! And while this trend disproves concerns that regulators can't keep up with the pace of change, it also provides an opportunity to take better advantage of that change.

Assumption: Technology Will Be Used as a Tool of Obstruction

Often, rapid technological developments are perceived as potential tools of obstruction, allowing authoritarian leaders to control access to information and thereby cementing their own power, allowing them to continue to restrict human rights in those countries where they're in power. Consider, for instance, China's Great Firewall, or recently Vladimir Putin's ability to shut down the website of his main political opponent, Alexei Navalny.[121]

It's true: people in positions of power often have the ability to regulate the influence of digital technology in their societies, controlling the flow of information and restricting certain forms of expression. One of the most popular scenarios to cite is Orwell's *1984*, a dystopian story in which the government, in the form of Big Brother, monitors and controls information and communication to such a degree that it maintains a stranglehold over the state, holding an entire population in its thrall.

Though such an argument reflects a slight misreading of Orwell in the first place, it's important to recognize such a dystopian conclusion to the story of development is far from certain in the first place. Indeed, society's best defenses against autocratic control come from the very technology that such detractors fear and its ability to empower individuals and entire societies to *overcome* forms of technological oppression.

Before examining the ability of technology to overcome those who would use it for purposes of oppression, it's worth noting the inherent contradiction between this misconception and the argument I discussed earlier concerning regulatory powers. If one believes technology's advance is too powerful to be regulated, then it's illogical to assert that other government agencies would have the ability to harness technology so effectively they could use it to hold sway over an entire population. This type of cognitive dissonance is emblematic of an approach that tends too often to ask the wrong questions. We shouldn't be thinking, *What can we do about technology?* Instead, we should be asking ourselves, indeed, with a measure of awe, *What can technology do?*

Often, the answer is right in front of us, even if we don't recognize it for what it is. While many are concerned about governments using technological power to suppress opposition, we can see exactly the opposite occurring: technology, in the hands of ordinary people, enables them to do extraordinary things. One of the most powerful social movements of the new century occurred in the Middle East and North Africa, where it enabled protesters to communicate and coordinate with smartphones, on social media, and through livestreams and real-time updates. Technology helped make the Arab Spring possible, ousting dictators throughout the region. This is evidence of technology's unique ability to unite people, and it flies in the face of technological skepticism that often claims the opposite.[122]

Along similar lines, new conversations are playing out around the world about the role technology plays in politics. Though many of the political themes at work in debates about the role and impact of digital technology are interrelated, there's a sharp divide between conversations about the role of technology in the politics of *resistance* versus the role of technology in the politics of *participation*. Though the ideal ends are often the same—stable, informed democracies—the means of attaining them are different, coming from authoritarian contexts as opposed to democratic ones. As I pointed out earlier, technology in authoritarian settings doesn't empower leaders to suppress populations, it empowers populations to overcome suppression. The arguments here are drawn along similar lines. People who tend to be concerned about the impacts of technology in democracies often cite a more divided population. News delivered via social media can reinforce preexisting beliefs, adding to the so-called bubble effect that has recently attained particular prominence in US news during and after the 2016 presidential election.

While it's very likely true social media played a role in creating a more polarized political environment, it reflects a low-value questioning approach to imagine that technological developments bear responsibility for negative outcomes. Indeed, new thinking suggests not only that the role of social media in political polarization is overstated, but, more importantly, continuing to develop the technology can provide solutions, and indeed net humanistic positives, to a problematic status quo. Taking a high-value questioning approach to the issue of technology's effects in democracies reveals several areas where the human impact of new technology is profound.

Digital technology promotes the functional elements of democracy, which is itself a humanistic good. Democracy as a political and social system places an emphasis not only on the rights, but the value of the individual, highlighting individual human potential as an ideal that a democratic system can maximize. Democracy tends to protect human rights rather than suppress them. Democracy tends to enable humans to achieve their goals rather than prevent them. Democracy tends to promote conditions for human success in culture as well as politics rather than marginalize them. For all of these reasons, democracy itself is a humanistic goal, and to whatever extent digital technology can help achieve, promote, and sustain it, that technology is promoting a humanistic end.

One major effect digital technology has on the function of democracy is increasing voter participation. Very simply, it can make voting easier, as well as allow more people to vote. Digital processes and registries can make voting registration, a process that's often arduous, far easier. Rather than filling out paper forms, driving to destinations, waiting in lines, and generally taking up time and causing a hassle, streamlined voter registration can have the simple and immediate impact of improving voter turnout, something nearly universally regarded as a net positive in democratic systems.[123]

Beyond registration, voting itself can be made simpler and easier through technological innovation. Studies demonstrate that complex voting systems can suppress voter turnout, particularly among elderly voters who might not easily understand the process. However, technological development isn't the same as increasing complexity. Rather, it can have the opposite effect, making interfaces much simpler and easier to use. This directly overcomes the voting obstacle posed by complexity, making political participation more attractive.[124]

Political participation, however, is more than just showing up at the ballot box. In a pluralist society, just as important as the voters are the candidates themselves, as well as the field they play on. New evolutions in digital technology flatten the political playing field in a variety of ways, most importantly by making platforms, ideas, and candidacies more accessible. Technological developments have always had a profound democratic impact on society. Once upon a time, newspapers were the only way for leaders and candidates to reach their constituents. Then, FDR took the revolutionary step of broadcasting his Fireside Chats on the radio during his presidency, bringing his message directly to the people. John F. Kennedy did the same in the first televised debate between presidential candidates, allowing voters access to the election process that, up to that point, they had never had before. Now, in the twenty-first century, we bear witness to the tremendous impact the internet has on democratic political participation.

The internet allows individuals to be front and center on every issue and take part in every debate, informing themselves and their fellow citizens along the way. They have direct access to speeches and policy positions of every candidate, and they can inform themselves whenever suits them. Likewise, candidates for office and elected representatives have the opportunity to reach every voter with an internet connection, highlighting the messages and platforms that are important to them.

Further, online participation has the profound effect of leveling the financial playing field in politics. In an era characterized, up until now, by the overwhelming presence of big money in politics, when super PACs and megadonors have outsize impacts on elections by buying messaging and ad time, the internet allows an unprecedented opportunity for candidates without these advantages to enter the arena by crowdfunding their campaign donations. Bernie Sanders made history by outraising his opponent primarily with smaller donations from around the country. Regardless of your political beliefs, leanings, or candidates of preference, a level playing field and a plurality of candidates is a necessary part of a vibrant democracy with humanistic benefits, and it's promoted in no small measure by quickly developing technology.[125]

Another major reason for concern about spreading technological development is the ability of authoritarian governments to restrict it or manipulate it for their own ends to suppress freedom of expression. This is closely related to the idea of communication and coordination I just discussed, but it's also different in crucial ways. While it's just as important as promoting coordination with the goal of achieving traditionally understood human rights, technology itself is playing a role in changing our understanding of human rights for the better.[126]

The digital era has ushered in an entirely new conversation about human rights with an inclusive, broad approach that leads us towards enshrining new values as worthy of the status of human rights. This type of progress is part of the natural tendency of technological advancement driving humanitarian progress, forcing us to develop a more comprehensive understanding of the rights to which all humans are entitled. The digital age's unique contribution to this discussion has been the right of access to information. The link between this new understanding of human rights and technology is significant because of its progressive effect. It allows us to recognize the *need* for a reexamination of human rights that allows societies to take the steps necessary for securing them, improving the station and condition of people around the world.

UNESCO—the arm of the United Nations concerned with education, science, and culture—affirmed an expansion on the fundamental right of Freedom of Information in 2010. Freedom of Information, as a broad part of the human rights canon, no longer simply means freedom of expression and freedom from censorship.[127] It's not merely a negative right anymore, but a positive one: our very *access* to information ought to be guaranteed. This would have been unthinkable before the internet provided societies around the world with ubiquitous information access. Our understanding of that right has evolved along with the technology that helps us achieve it.

Technology Drives the Ultimate Humanistic Value: The Creation of Knowledge

One of the most fundamental and valuable elements of a humanist approach is the creation and the spreading of knowledge. Think back to original humanistic roots in the Renaissance, characterized by a passionate endeavor to discover as much as possible about the human condition through every means: art, literature, poetry, exploration, and scientific discovery. More than anything else, golden ages in human history are characterized by attempts toward, increases of, and celebration of knowledge: the human pursuit of understanding ourselves and our world. While I focused earlier on the European Renaissance because of its generation of the humanistic concept, I want to take a moment to emphasize that golden ages are not restricted to any part of the world or any time period. They're found anywhere a priority is placed on scientific development, because that development allows us to improve the status, condition, and quality of life of our fellow human beings. Europe's Renaissance and scientific revolution are justifiably honored. But so was the golden age of Islam, which saw the development of mathematics and calculus, and the golden age of China during the Tang Dynasty, which saw great leaps in medicine, machinery, and cartography.

The golden age of India during the Gupta empire was driven by progress in mathematics and astronomy. There are vastly many more. Every civilization celebrates a time when the pace and the quality of science and knowledge creation outstrip any other in their history.

The convergence of technological advancement, economic progress, and cultural enrichment is no coincidence. What do all three things have in common? An emphasis on the human spirit. History is our best guide, and it tells us not to fear technological change, but to embrace it. In this digital age, we should let technology lift the human spirit in a celebration of Digital Humanism.

Q	What impact will rapid technological change have on democracy?
B	A healthy democracy is best served by universal access to information.
A	1. Prioritize internet access in rural areas. 2. Publicize voting information, including times and locations. 3. Ensure access to content behind paywalls.
M	1. Measure voter registration 2. Measure voter participation

Table 8: QBAM for Technology's Effect on Democracy

When I think about Questioneering and what it means to be a good Questioneer, I envision someone who understands that it's not about what you know, but about what you share. It's your ability to ultimately create an environment that allows and accelerates the ability for people to share, to stay in the moment, to stay focused, and become emotionally connected, so they're able to ask high-level questions.

When you inspire the level of emotional connection your employees, friends, and associates need to drive forward, they'll persevere through the most difficult challenges they'll invariably face. It's truly not about the destination, but about the ride. Your ability to go from low-value to high-value questions is truly the only sustainable piece of competitive differentiation in the digital age.

Moving from low-value to high-value questions in a frictionless manner is the single most defining moment of sustainable, competitive differentiation you can have in the digital age, whether you're the leader of a 75,000-person company or an individual contributor, independent contractor, or entrepreneur. Your ability to move from low value to high value, the inclusive culture that you drive and you build around you, is your truly sustainable advantage.

I hope you've enjoyed this book and the conversation we've had. Remember, Questioneering is all about challenging what you believe to be true to ultimately drive your success.

We've all been taught there's no such thing as a bad question. But that mindset perpetuates an attitude of laziness where we don't spend enough time on thoroughly considering the question. All things are important, but they're not equal. And while there may not be such a thing as a bad question, there's definitely such a thing as a low- and high-value question. Your goal is to seek high-value questions because high-value questions lead to high-value answers, which lead to breakthrough innovations.

I wish you good luck on your quest and the very best in becoming one of the world's premier Questioneering experts.

P.S. In the spirit of inclusion, I'd like to welcome you to my Questioneering community. It's fun, always surprising, and filled with the coolest questions that keep getting better. Come join now at www.questioneering. net. Once you join, you'll get my list of Top 15 Common Questions broken down by the steps of the ASK process: Aim, Surprise, and Kindle.

P.P.S. Did you like this book? Whether you answered yes or no, please consider visiting Amazon, searching for Questioneering, and giving the book a review. It means the world to me! Thank you!

Notes

1 "2012 Cisco Connected World Technology Report," Cisco Systems, December 12, 2012, https://newsroom.cisco.com/feature-content?articleId=1114851.

2 Christina DesMarais, "30 CEOs Reveal the Daily Habits Responsible for Their Success," Inc., September 18, 2015, https://www.inc.com/christina-desmarais/30-ce-os-reveal-the-daily-habits-responsible-for-their-success.html.

3 Christina DesMarais, "30 CEOs Reveal the Daily Habits Responsible for Their Success," Inc., September 18, 2015, https://www.inc.com/christina-desmarais/30-ce-os-reveal-the-daily-habits-responsible-for-their-success.html.

4 Christine Liao, "Rapid Prototyping Google Glass," San Francisco Design Week, April 13, 2016, https://2018.sfdesignweek.org/rapid-prototyping-google-glass/.

5 "John Ciardi Quotes," BrainyQuote.com, February 2, 2018, https://www.brainyquote.com/quotes/john_ciardi_402193.

6 Heather Clancy, "Joseph Bradley, Cisco: Imagine Your Internet of Everything," GreenBiz, March 13, 2018, https://www.greenbiz.com/blog/2014/03/25/how-make-case-your-internet-everything-vision.

7 Howard Tiersky, "5 Top Challenges to Digital Transformation in the Enterprise," CIO, March 13, 2017, https://www.cio.com/article/3179607/e-commerce/5-top-challenges-to-digital-transformation-in-the-enterprise.html.

8 The Build Network Staff, "You Cannot Solve What You Don't Understand," Inc., May 19, 2013, https://www.inc.com/thebuildnetwork/you-cannot-solve-what-you-dont-understand.html.

9 Thea Singer, "The Innovation Factor: Your Brain on Innovation," Inc., September 1, 2002, https://www.inc.com/magazine/20020901/24544.

10 Ben Sisario, "With a Tap of Taylor Swift's Fingers, Apple Retreated," The New York Times, June 22, 2015, https://www.nytimes.com/2015/06/23/business/media/as-quick-as-a-taylor-swift-tweet-apple-had-to-change-its-tune.html.

11 Ben Sisario, "Taylor Swift Criticism Spurs Apple to Change Royalties Policy," The New York Times, June 21, 2015, https://www.nytimes.com/2015/06/22/business/media/taylor-swift-criticizes-apples-terms-for-streaming-music-service.html.

12 "IDC Digital Universe Study: Big Data, Bigger Digital Shadows and Biggest Growth in the Far East," EMC Corporation, December 11, 2012, http://www.

whizpr.be/upload/medialab/21/company/media_presentation_2012_digiuniverse-final1.pdf.

[13] *Star Wars IV: A New Hope*. Written and Directed by George Lucas. (1977; Beverly Hills, CA: 20th Century Fox Home Entertainment, 2013), DVD.

[14] Alan Zorfas and Daniel Leemon, "An Emotional Connection Matters More Than Customer Satisfaction," Harvard Business Review, August 29, 2016, https://hbr.org/2016/08/an-emotional-connection-matters-more-than-customer-satisfaction.

[15] Amy Feldmon, "Ten of the Most Successful Companies Built on Kickstarter," Forbes, April 14, 2016, https://www.forbes.com/sites/amyfeldman/2016/04/14/ten-of-the-most-successful-companies-built-on-kickstarter/#5661a8e569e8.

[16] "Welcome to Medium. Where Words Matter," Medium, 2018, https://medium.com/about.

[17] "Welcome to Medium. Where Words Matter," Medium, 2018, https://medium.com/about.

[18] Deanna Ting, "Airbnb's Latest Investment Values It as Much as Hilton and Hyatt Combined," Skift, September 23, 2016, https://skift.com/2016/09/23/airbnbs-latest-investment-values-it-as-much-as-hilton-and-hyatt-combined/.

[19] Kevin McSpadden, "You Now Have a Shorter Attention Span Than a Goldfish," Time, May 14, 2015, http://time.com/3858309/attention-spans-goldfish/.

[20] Constantinos-Vasilios Priporas, Nikolaos Stylos, and Anestis K. Fotiadis, "Generation Z Consumers' Expectations of Interactions in Smart Retailing: A Future Agenda," Science Direct, January 31, 2017, https://www.sciencedirect.com/science/article/pii/S0747563217300729.

[21] "2015 Cone Communications Millennial CSR Study," Cone Communications, 2015, http://www.conecomm.com/research-blog/2015-cone-communications-millennial-csr-study#download-research.

[22] "Trump Again Blames Both Sides for Virginia, Reigniting a Political Firestorm," Reuters, Fortune, August 16, 2016, http://fortune.com/2017/08/16/trump-charlottesville-virginia-white-supremacists-crisis-race/.

[23] Laura A. Hymson, "The Company That Taught the World to Sing: Coca-Cola, Globalization, and the Cultural Politics of Branding in the Twentieth Century," The University of Michigan, 2011, https://deepblue.lib.umich.edu/bitstream/handle/2027.42/86471/lhymson_1.pdf.

[24] Tom Batchelor and Christopher Hooton, "Pepsi Advert with Kendall Jenner Pulled After Huge Backlash," Independent, April 5, 2017, http://www.independent.co.uk/arts-entertainment/tv/news/pepsi-advert-pulled-kendall-jenner-protest-video-cancelled-removed-a7668986.html.

[25] Eli Meixler, "Dodge's Super Bowl Ad Using Martin Luther King's Voice Is Not Going Down Well," Time, February 5, 2018, http://time.com/5132811/martin-luther-king-dodge-ram-super-bowl-commercial/.

[26] Josh Hafner, "That Martin Luther King Jr. Speech Used in Ram's Car ad? It Goes on to Criticize Car Ads," USA Today, February 5, 2018, https://www.usatoday.com/story/news/nation-now/2018/02/05/mlk-speech-used-rams-car-ad-goes-criticize-car-ads/306984002/.

[27] "2015 Cone Communications Millennial CSR Study," Cone Communications, 2015, http://www.conecomm.com/research-blog/2015-cone-communications-millennial-csr-study#download-research.

[28] Main Sami, "Podcast Revenue Will Jump 85% This Year to Hit $220 Million," Adweek, June 26, 2017, http://www.adweek.com/digital/podcast-revenue-will-jump-85-this-year-to-hit-220-million/.

[29] Pete Vernon, "Q&A: Former Obama Staffers Launch Crooked Media," CJR, January 13, 2017, https://www.cjr.org/covering_trump/crooked_media_trump.php.

[30] Jim Rutenberg, "Opposition and a Shave: Former Obama Aides Counter Trump," March 20, 2017, https://www.nytimes.com/2017/03/20/business/media/rutenberg-trump-opposition-pod-save-america.html.

[31] "2015 Cone Communications Millennial CSR Study," Cone Communications, 2015, http://www.conecomm.com/research-blog/2015-cone-communications-millennial-csr-study#download-research.

[32] "2015 Cone Communications Millennial CSR Study," Cone Communications, 2015, http://www.conecomm.com/research-blog/2015-cone-communications-millennial-csr-study#download-research.

[33] Ryan Rudominer, "CSR Matters: Now Is the Time for Purpose-Driven Companies to Lead," Accessed Feb 17, 2018, http://csic.georgetown.edu/magazine/csr-matters-now-time-purpose-driven-companies-lead/.

[34] Tessa Stuart, "Inside the Bill O'Reilly Advertiser Boycott," Rolling Stone, April 6, 2017, https://www.rollingstone.com/politics/features/inside-the-bill-oreilly-advertiser-boycott-w475352.

35 Matthew Ingram, "More Advertisers Boycott Fox News Show after Harassment Allegations," April 4, 2017, http://fortune.com/2017/04/04/ad-boycott-fox-news/.

36 "Corporate BDS," The Lawfare Project, Accessed February 15, 2018, https://thelawfareproject.org/discrimination-bds/corporatebds/.

37 Glen Greenwald, "U.S. Lawmakers Seek to Criminally Outlaw Support for Boycott Campaign against Israel," July 19, 2017, https://theintercept.com/2017/07/19/u-s-lawmakers-seek-to-criminally-outlaw-support-for-boycott-campaign-against-israel/.

38 Niv Elis, "When BDS and Corporate Social Responsibility Collide," June 12, 2015, http://www.jpost.com/Business-and-Innovation/When-BDS-and-corporate-social-responsibility-collide-405817.

39 "New Report on Campuses and Endowments Investing in Clean Energy," International Endowments Network, November 2, 2016, http://www.intentionalendowments.org/clean_energy_white_paper_press_release.

40 "Trump's Executive Order: Who Does Travel Ban Affect?" BBC, February 10, 2017, http://www.bbc.com/news/world-us-canada-38781302.

41 Raz Godelnik, "Reframing Corporate Responsibility: The New Rules for the Trump Era," Parsons School of Design, Accessed February 14, 2018, http://sds.parsons.edu/designmanagement/reframing-corporate-responsibility-the-new-rules-for-the-trump-era/.

42 Gianluca Mezzofiore, "Starbucks CEO's Powerful Open Letter on Trump's Muslim Ban," Mashable, January 30, 2017, https://mashable.com/2017/01/30/starbucks-muslim-ban-trump-open-letter/#tOzFi1PpkkqX.

43 Brian Fung and Herman Wong, "'Apple Would Not Exist without Immigration:' Companies at Trump's Tech Summit React to His Travel Ban." The Washington Post, January 29, 2017, https://www.washingtonpost.com/news/wonk/wp/2017/01/29/apple-would-not-exist-without-immigration-companies-at-trumps-tech-summit-react-to-his-travel-ban/?utm_term=.b9d1a4b4bcaf.

44 T.C. Sottek, "Netflix CEO: 'Trump's Actions Are So Un-American It Pains Us All,'" The Verge, January 28, 2017, https://www.theverge.com/2017/1/28/14426536/netflix-reed-hastings-trump-immigration-executive-order.

45 T.C. Sottek, "Netflix CEO: 'Trump's Actions Are So Un-American It Pains Us All,'" The Verge, January 28, 2017, https://www.theverge.com/2017/1/28/14426536/netflix-reed-hastings-trump-immigration-executive-order.

[46] Keon Kaye, "Lyft Stands Up to Trump and the Refugee Ban, While Uber Stumbles," Triple pundit, February 1, 2017, https://www.triplepundit.com/2017/02/lyft-uber-trump-refugee-muslim-ban/.

[47] Amy Nordrum, "Popular Internet of Things Forecast of 50 Billion Devices by 2020 Is Outdated," IEEE Spectrum, August 18, 2016, https://spectrum.ieee.org/tech-talk/telecom/internet/popular-internet-of-things-forecast-of-50-billion-devices-by-2020-is-outdated.

[48] Trips Reddy, "7 Big Data Blunders You're Thankful Your Company Didn't Make," Umbel, October 22, 2014, https://www.umbel.com/blog/big-data/7-big-data-blunders.

[49] "Consumer Expectation Versus Business Reality," Experian, https://www.edq.com/globalassets/uk/papers/consumer-expectations-versus-business-reality.pdf. p. 4.

[50] "Driver's License, Credit Card Numbers: The Equinox Hack Is Way Worse Than Consumers Knew," CNBC, February 12, 2018, https://www.cnbc.com/2018/02/12/the-equifax-hack-is-way-worse-than-consumers-knew.html.

[51] Pat Conroy, Frank Milano, Anupam Narula, and Raj Singhal, "Building Consumer Trust: Protecting Personal Data in the Consumer Product Industry," Deloitte University, 2014, https://www2.deloitte.com/content/dam/insights/us/articles/consumer-data-privacy-strategies/DUP_970-Building-consumer-trust_MASTER.pdf. p. 5.

[52] "Consumer Expectation Versus Business Reality," Experian, https://www.edq.com/globalassets/uk/papers/consumer-expectations-versus-business-reality.pdf. p. 7.

[53] "MEF Global Consumer Trust Report 2017: Consumer Insights to Understand the Impact, Challenges and Opportunities of Building Trust in Personal Data." Mobile Ecosystem Forum, June 2017, https://mobileecosystemforum.com/wp-content/uploads/2017/06/MEF_Global_Consumer_Trust_Report_2017.pdf. pp. 7–8.

[54] Pat Conroy, Frank Milano, Anupam Narula, and Raj Singhal, "Building Consumer Trust: Protecting Personal Data in the Consumer Product Industry," Deloitte University, 2014, https://www2.deloitte.com/content/dam/insights/us/articles/consumer-data-privacy-strategies/DUP_970-Building-consumer-trust_MASTER.pdf. p. 9.

[55] "Using Personal Data to Build Customer Trust and Competitive Advantage," PwC, February 2, 2017. http://pwc.blogs.com/analytics_means_business/2017/02/using-personal-data-to-build-customer-trust-and-competitive-advantage.html.

[56] "Consumer Expectation Versus Business Reality," Experian, https://www.edq.com/globalassets/uk/papers/consumer-expectations-versus-business-reality.pdf. p. 4.

[57] "The Four V's of Big Data." IBM Big Data & Analytics Hub, Accessed February 15, 2018, http://www.ibmbigdatahub.com/infographic/four-vs-big-data.

[58] Gil Press, "6 Predictions for the $203 Billion Big Data Analytics Market," Forbes, January 20, 2017, https://www.forbes.com/sites/gilpress/2017/01/20/6-predictions-for-the-203-billion-big-data-analytics-market/#19a10e412083.

[59] ""The Four V's of Big Data." IBM Big Data & Analytics Hub, Accessed February 15, 2018, http://www.ibmbigdatahub.com/infographic/four-vs-big-data.

[60] Thomas Redman, "Bad Data Costs the U.S. $3 Trillion Per Year," Forbes, September 22, 2016, https://hbr.org/2016/09/bad-data-costs-the-u-s-3-trillion-per-year.

[61] Tadhg Nagle, Thomas C. Redman, and David Sammon, "Only 3% of Companies' Data Meets Basic Quality Standards," Harvard Business Review, September 11, 2017, https://hbr.org/2017/09/only-3-of-companies-data-meets-basic-quality-standards.

[62] Trips Reddy, "7 Big Data Blunders You're Thankful Your Company Didn't Make," Umbel, October 22, 2014, https://www.umbel.com/blog/big-data/7-big-data-blunders.

[63] Pitney Bowes, "The Data Differentiator: How Improving Data Quality Improves Business," Forbes Insights, May 2017, https://www.forbes.com/forbesinsights/pitney_bowes_data_quality/index.html. p. 5.

[64] Pitney Bowes, "The Data Differentiator: How Improving Data Quality Improves Business," Forbes Insights, May 2017, https://www.forbes.com/forbesinsights/pitney_bowes_data_quality/index.html. pp. 10–13.

[65] "Now or Never: 2016 Global CEO Outlook," KPMG International, June 2016, https://home.kpmg.com/content/dam/kpmg/pdf/2016/06/2016-global-ceo-outlook.pdf. p. 10.

[66] Pitney Bowes, "The Data Differentiator: How Improving Data Quality Improves Business," Forbes Insights, May 2017, https://www.forbes.com/forbesinsights/pitney_bowes_data_quality/index.html. pp. 10–12.

[67] "Bad Data Costs United Airlines $1B Annually," Travel Data Daily, February 16, 2018, https://www.traveldatadaily.com/bad-data-costs-united-airlines-1b-annually.

[68] J.P. Mangalindan, "Why Amazon's Fire Phone Failed," Fortune, September 29, 2014, http://fortune.com/2014/09/29/why-amazons-fire-phone-failed/.

[69] Ethan Wolff-Mann, "A Sweeping Regulation Will Change How Europe Uses the Internet," Yahoo Finance, February 15, 2018, https://finance.yahoo.com/news/sweeping-regulation-will-change-europe-uses-internet-190130093.html.

[70] "Consumer Expectation Versus Business Reality," Experian, https://www.edq.com/globalassets/uk/papers/consumer-expectations-versus-business-reality.pdf. p. 7.

[71] Kate Clark, "The Top Venture Capital Investors in Cryptocurrency Startups," PitchBook, December 12, 2017, https://pitchbook.com/news/articles/the-top-venture-capital-investors-in-cryptocurrency-startups.

[72] "Lockheed Martin Contracts Guardtime Federal for Innovative Cyber Technology," Lockheed Martin, April 27, 2017, https://news.lockheedmartin.com/2017-04-27-Lockheed-Martin-Contracts-Guardtime-Federal-for-Innovative-Cyber-Technology.

[73] "Deep Shift: Technology Tipping Points and Societal Impact," World Economic Forum, September 2015, http://www3.weforum.org/docs/WEF_GAC15_Technological_Tipping_Points_report_2015.pdf. p. 24.

[74] IBM Blockchain Unleashed, "Blockchain in Healthcare: Patient Benefits and More," IBM, October 23, 2017, https://www.ibm.com/blogs/blockchain/2017/10/blockchain-in-healthcare-patient-benefits-and-more.

[75] IBM Blockchain Unleashed, "Blockchain in Healthcare: Patient Benefits and More," IBM, October 23, 2017, https://www.ibm.com/blogs/blockchain/2017/10/blockchain-in-healthcare-patient-benefits-and-more.

[76] "Report: Medical Record Mix-ups Are a Common Problem," NPR, October 1, 2016, https://www.npr.org/2016/10/01/496195979/report-medical-record-mix-ups-are-a-common-problem.

[77] PR Newswire, "Blockchain Market to Grow at a CAGR of 61.5% by 2021: BFSI Sector Is Expected to Dominate the Market During the Forecast Period—Research and Markets." The Street, June 7, 2017, https://www.thestreet.com/story/14169220/1/blockchain-market-to-grow-at-a-cagr-of-615-by-2021-bfsi-sector-is-expected-to-dominate-the-market-during-the-forecast-period--research-and-markets.html.

[78] Technologent, "The Growth of Edge Computing and Its Impact on IT Strategy," Technologent, August 14, 2017, https://blog.technologent.com/the-growth-of-edge-computing-and-its-impact-on-it-strategy.

[79] "Gartner Reveals Top Predictions for IT Organizations and Users in 2018 and Beyond," Gartner, October 3, 2017, https://www.gartner.com/newsroom/id/3811367.

[80] "Using Personal Data to Build Customer Trust and Competitive Advantage," PwC, February 2, 2017, http://pwc.blogs.com/analytics_means_business/2017/02/using-personal-data-to-build-customer-trust-and-competitive-advantage.html.

[81] Michael Meyers, "Four Dirty Data Horror Stories—When Good Data Goes Bad," LinkedIn, December 10, 2014, https://www.linkedin.com/pulse/dirty-data-horror-stories-when-michael/.

[82] Pat Conroy, Frank Milano, Anupam Narula, and Raj Singhal, "Building Consumer Trust: Protecting Personal Data in the Consumer Product Industry," Deloitte University, 2014, https://www2.deloitte.com/content/dam/insights/us/articles/consumer-data-privacy-strategies/DUP_970-Building-consumer-trust_MASTER.pdf. p. 14–20.

[83] Bud Bilanich, "Why You Must Define Your Own Career Success," Bud Blianich Blog, http://www.budbilanich.com/define-career-success/.

[84] Steve Denning, "What Does 'Career Success' Really Mean?" Forbes, March 14, 2016, https://www.forbes.com/sites/stevedenning/2016/03/14/what-does-career-success-really-mean/#66badf677cf5.

[85] Douglas Coupland, *Generation X: Tales for an Accelerated Culture* (New York: St. Martin's Press, 1991).

[86] Rieva Lesonsky, "How to Retain Gen X Employees and Why You Want To," Small Business Trends, March 16, 2016, https://smallbiztrends.com/2016/05/how-to-retain-gen-x-employees.html.

[87] Rieva Lesonsky, "How to Retain Gen X Employees and Why You Want To," Small Business Trends, March 16, 2016, https://smallbiztrends.com/2016/05/how-to-retain-gen-x-employees.html.

[88] Kim Cassady, "3 Ways Technology Influences Generational Divides at Work," Entrepreneur, March 28, 2017, https://www.entrepreneur.com/article/290763.

[89] Kevin Kruse, "How to Harness the Power of a Millennial Workforce," Forbes, May 11, 2017, https://www.forbes.com/sites/kevinkruse/2017/05/11/how-to-harness-the-power-of-a-millennial-workforce/#46a4fa84382b.

[90] "The 2016 Deloitte Millennial Survey Winning Over the Next Generation of Leaders," Deloitte Consulting, 2016, https://www2.deloitte.com/content/dam/Deloitte/global/Documents/About-Deloitte/gx-millenial-survey-2016-exec-summary.pdf.

[91] Sarah Landrum, "How Millennials Are Changing How We View Success," Forbes, December 30, 2016, https://www.forbes.com/sites/sarahlandrum/2016/12/30/how-millennials-are-changing-how-we-view-success/#534c92d43b94.

[92] Ryan Jenkins, Inc., "Forget Millennials—Here Are 8 Things You'll Want to Remember about Gen Z," Business Insider. July 24, 2017, http://www.businessinsider.com/forget-millennials-here-are-8-things-to-know-about-gen-z-2017-7.

[93] Richard Madison, "What to Expect from Gen Z: The New Grads Entering the Workforce in 2016," Brighton School of Business and Management, https://universitybusiness.co.uk/Article/what-to-expect-from-gen-z.

[94] Richard Madison, "What to Expect from Gen Z: The New Grads Entering the Workforce in 2016," Brighton School of Business and Management, https://universitybusiness.co.uk/Article/what-to-expect-from-gen-z.

[95] Terry Dockery, "Performance Inputs Vs. Outputs," Business Psychology, April 12, 2012, http://www.businesspsychology.com/147/.

[96] Matthew Murray, "Inputs vs. Output: Do You Know What's Really Driving Your Sales?" The Center for Sales Strategy, October 5, 2016, http://blog.thecenterforsalesstrategy.com/inputs-vs.-output-do-you-know-whats-really-driving-your-sales.

[97] "Workforce of the Future: The Competing Forces Shaping 2030," PwC, 2017, https://www.pwc.com/gx/en/services/people-organisation/workforce-of-the-future/workforce-of-the-future-the-competing-forces-shaping-2030-pwc.pdf.

[98] "Workforce of the Future: The Competing Forces Shaping 2030," PwC, 2017, https://www.pwc.com/gx/en/services/people-organisation/workforce-of-the-future/workforce-of-the-future-the-competing-forces-shaping-2030-pwc.pdf.

[99] "Workforce of the Future: The Competing Forces Shaping 2030," PwC, 2017, https://www.pwc.com/gx/en/services/people-organisation/workforce-of-the-future/workforce-of-the-future-the-competing-forces-shaping-2030-pwc.pdf.

[100] "Workforce of the Future: The Competing Forces Shaping 2030," PwC, 2017, https://www.pwc.com/gx/en/services/people-organisation/workforce-of-the-future/workforce-of-the-future-the-competing-forces-shaping-2030-pwc.pdf.

[101] "Workforce of the Future: The Competing Forces Shaping 2030," PwC, 2017, https://www.pwc.com/gx/en/services/people-organisation/workforce-of-the-future/workforce-of-the-future-the-competing-forces-shaping-2030-pwc.pdf.

[102] "Workforce of the Future: The Competing Forces Shaping 2030," PwC, 2017, https://www.pwc.com/gx/en/services/people-organisation/workforce-of-the-future/workforce-of-the-future-the-competing-forces-shaping-2030-pwc.pdf.

[103] "Majority of U.S. Employers Support Workplace Flexibility," WorldatWork, October 5, 2015, https://www.worldatwork.org/docs/worldatworkpressreleases/2015/majority-of-us-employers-support.html.

[104] "6 Trends That Will Define Workplace Flexibility in 2017," Fox Business, December 26, 2016, http://www.foxbusiness.com/features/6-trends-that-will-define-workplace-flexibility-in-2017.

[105] "Workforce of the Future: The Competing Forces Shaping 2030," PwC, 2017, https://www.pwc.com/gx/en/services/people-organisation/workforce-of-the-future/workforce-of-the-future-the-competing-forces-shaping-2030-pwc.pdf.

[106] "Workforce of the Future: The Competing Forces Shaping 2030," PwC, 2017, https://www.pwc.com/gx/en/services/people-organisation/workforce-of-the-future/workforce-of-the-future-the-competing-forces-shaping-2030-pwc.pdf.

[107] Mars Dorian, "You + Your Digital Persona: How to Create a Relationship That Impacts the Online World Awesomely," Mars Dorian, 2011, http://www.marsdorian.com/2011/01/digital-persona/.

[108] Andy Foote, "3 Stunningly Good LinkedIn Profile SUMMARIES," LinkedInsights, February 7, 2013, https://www.linkedinsights.com/3-stunningly-good-linkedin-profile-summaries/.

[109] "Enterprise Managed Attriution," Telos, 2018, https://www.telos.com/cyber-security/telos-ghost/applications/enterprise-managed-attribution/.

[110] "Spending Plan," Business Dictionary, 2018, http://www.businessdictionary.com/definition/spending-plan.html.

[111] Rebecca Harris, "The Loneliness Epidemic," Independent, March 30, 2015, http://www.independent.co.uk/life-style/health-and-families/features/the-loneliness-epidemic-more-connected-than-ever-but-feeling-more-alone-10143206.html.

[112] Carina Wolff, "The 6 Health Benefits of Being Social," Simplemost, 2017, https://www.simplemost.com/health-benefits-of-being-social/.

[113] Nathan Collier, "'Until We Can Manage Time, We Can Manage Nothing Else.' – Peter F. Drucker; 1909–2005," NSCBlog, February 2, 2012, http://www.nscblog.com/miscellaneous/%E2%80%9Cuntil-we-can-manage-time-we-can-manage-nothing-else-%E2%80%9D-%E2%80%94-peter-f-drucker-1909%E2%80%932005/.

[114] "Definition of Humanism," American Humanist Organization, 2018, https://americanhumanist.org/what-is-humanism/definition-of-humanism/.

[115] Martin Recke, "What Is Digital Humanism?" Next, November 11, 2017, https://nextconf.eu/2017/11/what-is-digital-humanism/.

[116] Erik Brynjolfsson and Tom Mitchell, "What Can Machine Learning Do? Workforce Implications," Science, December 22, 2017, http://science.sciencemag.org/content/358/6370/1530.

[117] Erik Brynjolfsson and Tom Mitchell, "What Can Machine Learning Do? Workforce Implications," Science, December 22, 2017, http://science.sciencemag.org/content/358/6370/1530.

[118] Martin Recke, "What Is Digital Humanism?" Next, November 11, 2017, https://nextconf.eu/2017/11/what-is-digital-humanism/.

[119] Midad Doueihi, "About Digital Humanism," INA Global, July 16, 2013, http://www.inaglobal.fr/en/ideas/article/about-digital-humanism.

[120] "Digital Regulation: The Key to Promoting Economic Growth," BBVA, February 12, 2016, https://www.bbva.com/en/digital-regulation-key-promoting-economic-growth/.

[121] Sabra Ayers, "Russia Blocks Opposition Leader's Website after He Refuses to Remove Videos about a Kremlin-Connected Oligarch," Los Angeles Times, February 15, 2018, http://www.latimes.com/world/europe/la-fg-russia-navalny-20180215-story.html.

[122] Loren Treisman, "Access to Information: Bridging the Digital Divide in Africa," The Guardian, January 24, 2014, https://www.theguardian.com/global-development-professionals-network/2014/jan/24/digital-divide-access-to-information-africa.

[123] Gary H. Roseman and E. Frank Stephenson, "The Effect of Voting Technology on Voter Turnout: Do Computers Scare the Eldery?" *Public Choice* 123, no. ½ (2005): http://www.jstor.org/stable/30026789.

[124] Fabrizio Gilardi, "Digital Democracy: How Digital Technology Is Changing Democracy and Its Study," University of Zurich, August 18, 2016, https://www.fabriziogilardi.org/resources/papers/Digital-Democracy.pdf.

[125] Chris Megerian, "Bernie Sanders Rode Wave of Small Donations in Democratic Primary," Los Angeles Times, July 12, 2016, http://www.latimes.com/politics/la-na-trailguide-updates-bernie-sanders-rode-wave-of-small-1468337592-htmlstory.html.

[126] Roslyn Moore, "Using Digital Technologies for Freedom of Expression," DW Akademie, March 15, 2016, http://www.dw.com/en/using-digital-technologies-for-freedom-of-expression/a-19116226.

[127] "Freedom of Information," Unesco, 2017, http://www.unesco.org/new/en/communication-and-information/freedom-of-expression/freedom-of-information/.

CPSIA information can be obtained
at www.ICGtesting.com
Printed in the USA
LVOW13*0058300518
578943LV00012B/58/P